Michael Tippett

Michael Tippett
An introductory study

DAVID MATTHEWS

FABER AND FABER
London & Boston

First published in 1980
by Faber and Faber Limited
3 Queen Square London WC1 3AU
Printed in Great Britain by
Latimer Trend & Company Ltd, Plymouth
All rights reserved

British Library Cataloguing in Publication Data

Matthews, David
  Michael Tippett.
  1. Tippett, Sir Michael
  780'.92'4   ML410.T467

  ISBN 0–571–10954–3
  ISBN 0–571–11527–6 Pbk

TO MY MOTHER

Contents

Illustrations

Preface

The aim of this book is, in the first place, to provide an introduction to Tippett for those who enjoy his music and would like to know more about the composer and his work. As such the book is intentionally modest in size and scope. During the past twenty years, Tippett has emerged from comparative obscurity into wide recognition as a major composer, in America as well as in Britain and on the Continent. Most of his music has now been recorded, and scores are widely available, so that readers wishing to discover more about it will find no difficulty in doing so.

As a composer myself, I have found Tippett an inspiring figure, both as a man and as an artist. He has gone his own way, without regard to what has been considered fashionable, writing only those works he felt compelled to write. He has forged his own highly distinctive language out of what he loves best. A composer today has to create a personal tradition for himself if his work is to have anything more than ephemeral value; Tippett has, by his own example, shown us both how necessary this is and how it may be done. He has also shown, at a time when much contemporary music seems weighed down by an Oblomov-like inertia, that it is still possible to compose music of irrepressible energy and exuberance. The exuberance is infectious, it excites enthusiasm; and if I have managed to communicate some of the enthusiasm I feel for Tippett's music to the pages of this book, I shall be more than content.

April 1979   David Matthews

Acknowledgements

My grateful thanks are due to the following people: to David Stevens and Alan Woolgar of Schott & Co Ltd for much information and generous assistance; to Meirion Bowen, Judith Osborne, Robin Walker and Adolf Wood for valuable suggestions; to David Ayerst and Ian Kemp for biographical information; to Patrick Carnegy of Faber & Faber, who guided the book through its final stages; last, and certainly not least, to Sir Michael Tippett for his help and warm encouragement.

For permission to reproduce the illustrations, I should like to thank Commander Peter Kemp (Plate 1), Colin Matthews (4), Axel Poignant (6), Mrs Brenda Rogers (9, 10, by Houston Rogers), Uldis Saule (11), Schott & Co Ltd (3, 7, 8), Michael Ward and Times Newspapers Ltd (13), Fay Photo Service, Boston, Mass. (12), and the Radio Times Hulton Picture Library (5).

Quotations from the composer's writings are reproduced by kind permission of Sir Michael Tippett. Thanks are due to Schott & Co Ltd for all music examples from the composer's work, and to Boosey & Hawkes Ltd for quotations from Stravinsky's *The Rite of Spring* and Britten's Cello Symphony on pp. 26 and 78.

D.M.

CHAPTER ONE

Early Years

Michael Tippett has always been a countryman. He was born in a London nursing home on 2 January 1905; but in that same year his parents moved from Eastcote in Middlesex, on the outskirts of London, to the small Suffolk village of Wetherden, not far from Stowmarket, and it was there that he spent the formative years of his boyhood.

Wetherden is a peaceful, out-of-the-way place. The Tippetts lived in a sixteenth-century house on the edge of the village, a pleasantly rambling building, with some claim to legend: Queen Mary Tudor was supposed to have spent a night there on her way to Framlingham. Tippett's father added to the house an extension of his own design, and set into the outside wall a plaque of Rubens, a favourite painter. Adjoining the house is an old barn where Tippett used to play with his elder brother, Peter. House and barn remain today almost exactly as they were when the Tippetts lived there.

Tippett's father, Henry, was born in 1858. His family were Cornish, and Michael inherited his father's Celtic temperament and looks. By profession Henry was a lawyer; in politics and philosophical outlook a liberal rationalist of the Manchester School. Some shrewd financial investments—he had, for instance, been one of the backers of the Lyceum Theatre in London—enabled him to retire from the law while still comparatively young. By chance he acquired the ownership of a hotel in Cannes which he ran and improved. Swedish royalty stayed there, and he built the first hard tennis courts in the South of France, which still exist. He was clearly something of a creator. He loved music, and was possibly the more musical of the two parents. 'It was left to me to live my father's aspirations', Tippett has said.

His mother, Isabel, was some twenty years younger than her

husband. She was a remarkable woman of diverse talents. She wrote
and published some half-dozen novels in her youth and early middle-
age; she was an early, and active, member of the Labour Party, and an
ardent suffragette who went to prison for her beliefs, just as Tippett
himself was to do. Later she became a disciple of the theosophist
Rudolf Steiner and practised spiritual healing. Towards the end of her
life (she lived into her eighties) she took up painting. Whatever she did
was done with passion. She also played the piano and sang: Tippett
remembers her singing of a ballad by Roger Quilter as the first music
he heard.

He became interested in music at an early age, and at about the
same time as he started his schooling—mostly under the supervision of a
governess, though he walked to the nearby village of Woolpit to be
taught Latin—he also began to have weekly piano lessons from a local
teacher. From the age of eight or nine he conceived the idea of
becoming a composer, but of course without any real knowledge of
what this meant; nor did he make any practical attempts at writing
music. His musical experience was very limited, in a way hard to
imagine today: there was no radio, the range of music available on
gramophone records was small, and there were few opportunities for
him to hear music outside his home. He did not attend his first concert
until he was twelve, when an aunt took him to hear the young pianist
Benno Moiseiwitsch at the Queen's Hall in London.

At the age of nine he went to preparatory school in Dorset, and at
thirteen he was sent to a public school—Fettes College in Edinburgh.
He felt persecuted there and hated it. After two years he managed to
persuade his parents to let him leave; and he moved to Stamford
Grammar School in Lincolnshire, where he was much happier, and,
as he unblushingly recalls, 'a brilliant though somewhat wayward
and rebellious pupil'. The piano teacher at Stamford was called Mrs
Tinkler, and under her guidance his technique improved to such an
extent that he played a concerto in a school concert.

His father's involvement with the hotel in Cannes meant that his
parents lived a good deal of the time in France, and Tippett spent
most of his holidays there. His natural gift for languages enabled him to
become fluent in French by the age of ten. Later he was to acquire
equal mastery of German. Feeling thoroughly at home in these

languages has contributed to Tippett's European-ness, though his English roots have remained strong.

In 1919 his parents decided to sell the house at Wetherden and live permanently on the Continent, at first in France, then in Corsica and Italy. The physical link with Suffolk was broken, but it left an indelible impression on his mind and emotions: the childhood experience of the unspoilt English countryside in the years before the First World War gave him a grounding for life. And except for his time in London at the Royal College of Music, Tippett has never lived away from the country: it is there that he is truly at home.

The English creative imagination is deeply rooted in the countryside. This is as true of English music, since its renaissance at the end of the nineteenth century, as it is of painting and poetry: the English landscape has been as potent an extra-musical inspiration as the great Tudor and Jacobean composers have been a musical one. The outstanding English composers of the first part of this century—Elgar, Delius, Vaughan Williams, Holst—were all passionately attached to the countryside. (To a certain extent they shared a countryman's detachment from some of the main intellectual and political concerns of the day: one might even call them unsophisticated—certainly in comparison with such continental contemporaries as Mahler or Schoenberg; though this quality is, in fact, a source of their music's strength.) The lure of the countryside persisted for the next generation, so that even so cosmopolitan a figure as Britten was emphatically not a city-dweller, choosing to spend most of his life beside the Suffolk coast of his boyhood, and finding creative stimulus in its marshlands and grey seas. (Interestingly, the two dominating English composers of our time were brought up within forty miles of each other in the same county, though Britten's seaside town of Lowestoft was a quite different environment from Tippett's country village.)

Michael Tippett is just as cosmopolitan in outlook, and as intellectually far-ranging as any composer of this century. However, neither the fact that he is a countryman at heart, nor his relation to the pastoral tradition in English music, which at its deepest approaches nature mysticism, should be underestimated. There are passages in his music which evoke the 'sweet especial rural scene' as vividly as Elgar or

Vaughan Williams; passages (such as Ex. 1) perhaps redolent of the Suffolk landscape with its gently undulating horizons, wide skies and soft lights. But Tippett's music, unlike that of the previous generation, is not obviously nostalgic; there is no sense of loss, rather of a vision continually present.

Ex. 1   from *Fantasia on a Theme of Corelli*

CHAPTER TWO

The Music Student

In 1922, when he was seventeen, Tippett went with a school party to his first symphony concert. It was at the De Montfort Hall in Leicester, and the conductor was an old Stamfordian, Malcolm Sargent. The programme included Ravel's *Mother Goose* Suite, then still quite new. This concert made an overwhelming impression. The vague inclination towards composition that had been growing secretly and blindly inside him for many years now crystallized into certainty: he would become a composer, this would be his life's work. But how to learn composition? His first idea was to teach himself, and he found a copy of Sir Charles Stanford's book *Musical Composition*. The book begins with a discussion of harmony and counterpoint. According to Stanford, 'To speak of studying harmony and counterpoint is . . . to put the cart before the horse. It is counterpoint which develops harmony, and there is no such boundary-wall between the studies as most students imagine. . . . The first principle to be laid down is, therefore, to study counterpoint first, and through counterpoint to master harmony.' These words struck home; though Tippett hardly knew what counterpoint was, he knew instinctively that what Stanford said was right for him: his approach to composition should be through counterpoint. It was a decisive choice for his development as a composer.

To Tippett's parents, true members of the upper-middle class despite their unorthodoxies, the notion of music as a career just did not occur; it was not one of 'the professions'. They consulted Malcolm Sargent, who strongly advised against the idea of his becoming a composer. Nevertheless, with some reluctance, they agreed that he should go to the Royal College of Music. There he studied composition, first under Charles Wood, who, though he died shortly after Tippett entered the College, made a lasting impact on his development by introducing him to Beethoven. His next teacher was C. H. Kitson, an impeccably respectable composer who cast a cautious eye on Tippett's somewhat undisciplined attempts at academic exercises. He also learnt conducting from Malcolm Sargent and Adrian Boult.

At the time Tippett entered the College his practical knowledge of music had been very largely limited to a few piano pieces, while his technical knowledge was scanty. His years at the College were a great period of learning; but he benefited less from the formal instruction he got from his teachers than from suddenly being exposed to so much that was new to him. He began at last to acquire real experience of the whole range of the classical repertoire: Palestrina (the backbone of academic teaching); the English madrigalists; Bach, of course, but Handel even more; Mozart; and, above all, Beethoven. That first summer in London he regularly attended the Promenade Concerts at the Queen's Hall (where he cut a striking figure, immaculately dressed in white flannels, and usually carrying the appropriate miniature scores) and there he heard all the Beethoven symphonies for the first time; soon afterwards he heard the complete cycle of Beethoven string quartets played by the Lener Quartet. 'When I was a student', Tippett has written, 'I submitted entirely to the music of Beethoven. I explored his music so exhaustively that for a long time later on I listened to every other music but his.' But he eventually returned to Beethoven, who, as a man, represented for him an ideal in his attitude to life, and as a composer, an ideal model. All the dominant attributes of Beethoven's music, its dynamic energy, its all-embracing humanism, its passionate spiritual questing, are those of Tippett's too.

His enlightenment was by no means confined to music. He discovered the contemporary theatre; he read, and went to see, plays by Chekhov, Ibsen, Strindberg and Shaw. Shaw especially was a key figure in his intellectual development; and what appealed so strongly to the young Tippett was not so much Shaw's universally admired qualities of brilliant wit and prodigious craftsmanship as the central idea of his philosophy, his optimistic interpretation (notably in *Back to Methuselah*) of evolution as an intelligent process rather than as Darwin's blind and ignorant force. Tippett had found the idea of creative evolution before in Samuel Butler and Bergson (as had Shaw). Butler had been an early passion; new ones now and in the next few years were Goethe (he learnt German so that he might read him in the original), Yeats (whose use of language was strongly to influence his own literary style), and Frazer's *The Golden Bough*, which initiated him into the world of myth and symbol. All these different threads he drew together to formulate a coherent philosophy of his own.

He left the Royal College of Music, having obtained the degree of Bachelor of Music, in the summer of 1928. Now he had to decide how he would make his living, and where he would live. Most young artists who gravitate towards London tend to stay there until (if they are lucky) they have begun to make a name for themselves; Tippett knew that he must move back to the country where he would find the quiet he needed for composition, which he was now beginning to work at in earnest. The choice of place was not difficult, since he had already become the conductor of a concert and operatic society at Oxted in Surrey. He rented a cottage on a nearby farm, on the wooded slopes of the North Downs. Later his father gave him enough money to have a small house of his own built, near the one he had been renting.

In 1929 he obtained a part-time post at Hazelwood Preparatory School, near the adjacent town of Limpsfield, where he taught French and some music. The English master there was Christopher Fry (still a long way from fame as a poetic dramatist). He and Tippett became friends, and they collaborated in a number of the composer's early projects. After four years at the school Tippett decided to give up teaching, as it was becoming too much of a hindrance to composition.

Tippett later discarded all the music he wrote during those first years after leaving the Royal College of Music. It included two string quartets and a Concerto in D for small orchestra, songs for voice and piano, and a Psalm in C (*The Gateway*) for chorus and small orchestra with text by Christopher Fry. Though these pieces are immature, they contain plenty of good melodic ideas. His melodic gift was there from the start; but it took him a long time to acquire a composing technique to match.

With the local operatic society he undertook several productions at the Barn Theatre, Oxted, including Vaughan Williams's *The Shepherds of the Delectable Mountains* and his own realization of an eighteenth-century ballad opera, *The Village Opera*, for which he provided some new music and rescored the rest for the available chamber-orchestral forces. It was useful practical experience for a future composer of operas.

Another valuable experience was to hear a number of his chamber and orchestral pieces played at a concert at the Barn Theatre in April 1930. These performances, though they were well received and provoked an encouraging and perceptive review from a local critic, convinced Tippett that his composing technique was still far from adequate, and he decided he must have further tuition. He approached R. O. Morris, a composer and specialist in sixteenth-century counter-point, then on the staff of the Royal College of Music, who agreed to take him as a private pupil; and he embarked for the next eighteen months on a comprehensive and rigorous study of fugue. At the back of his mind may still have been Stanford's second principle for composi-tion: 'that the study of counterpoint, if it is to be of real value, must be strict'. Morris was just the sort of teacher Tippett needed. His approach to the study of counterpoint was indeed strict, but always creative, never pedantic. His own compositions, which are un-deservedly forgotten, combine contrapuntal mastery with considerable rhythmic freedom and invention. It is probably fair to say that Morris had the deepest influence of any living musician on Tippett's develop-ment, and it was after his period of study with Morris that he found his true direction as a composer.

CHAPTER THREE

Finding a Style

Living on his own in the country, Tippett was none the less acutely aware of and sensitive to the events of the larger world. It was only during the 1920s that he began to find out the truth about the First World War, which had meant little to him as a schoolboy beyond the image of soldiers marching gallantly off to the front singing patriotic songs. Discovering the reality—the millions of troops on both sides slaughtered in the trenches in futile battles for a few hundred yards of shell-blasted soil—was a profound shock. This, and the conviction that the 'land fit for heroes' which Lloyd George had promised to the returning troops was just empty rhetoric, led him to believe that only through socialism could another war be avoided and the mass of the people achieve real dignity. He read a number of books on political theory; and his temperament, his compassionate open-mindedness, made him susceptible to radical ideas. There were plenty of opportunities for him to talk over these ideas: he got to know some of the local trade-unionists, who would come round to his cottage on Sunday mornings for discussions; among his friends were members of left-wing groups modelled on the German *Wandervogel* movements (which were socialist—this was before Hitler came to power); while the members of his Oxted choir included a number of people with left-wing sympathies.

The great depression that followed the Wall Street Crash of 1929 affected Tippett deeply, and his ideas became less theoretical and more practical. When he gave up teaching, in 1932, he had to find some other way of supplementing his income, and so turned to conducting. He found two jobs which were connected with his growing interest in socialism. The first was to conduct the South London Orchestra for unemployed professional musicians, most of them recruited from cinema orchestras which had been disbanded when the 'talkies' replaced silent films at the end of the 1920s. The orchestra, which was run by the London County Council, was based at Morley College, the working-men's foundation in Southwark, and gave concerts in schools, churches, settlements, hospitals and parks, often with the participation of well-known soloists. It was a co-operative, with profits going to the players.

He also became director of two choirs run by the Education Department of the Royal Arsenal Co-operative Society, one at Abbey Wood near Woolwich, the other at New Malden in Surrey. These choirs gave performances of light opera. Tippett attempted to broaden their repertoire and (to some extent under the influence of the Marxist composer Alan Bush) to introduce music with a political flavour, though without much success.

Also in 1932 Tippett became involved with a particular group of victims of the economic slump. The ironstone mines at Boosbeck in the Cleveland district of North Yorkshire had been closed down and were not expected to re-open (they did, in fact, during the Second World War). A scheme was inaugurated to find work for the miners, and several work-camps were opened. Some of Tippett's friends were associated with this scheme. Tippett himself put on a performance of *The Beggar's Opera* for the miners with the Royal Arsenal Co-operative Society and local performers, and with his friend David Ayerst, who wrote the libretto, composed a ballad opera, *Robin Hood*, in which aristocratic power and oppression are trounced by the romantic hero of the people. This was performed at Boosbeck in 1933.

The music he wrote immediately after his studies with R. O. Morris shows a marked advance in technique, though the first two pieces—a String Trio and a Symphony—remain unpublished, as does the slightly later *A Song of Liberty*, a choral and orchestral setting of part of Blake's *The Marriage of Heaven and Hell*. The first piece which Tippett has wanted to publish, though in a rather different form from the one in which it was conceived, is the First String Quartet of 1934–5. In 1943 he replaced the original first two movements—an adagio and a scherzo—with a sonata allegro, a tense and passionate piece in his Beethoven manner. He felt that these two movements, though satisfying from a formal point of view, were not strong enough musically. In fact the revision makes an even more satisfying shape. The original contained two substantial slow movements; in the revised version these have been replaced, to considerably greater effect, by a single slow movement, placed centrally. This movement presents three varied statements of an enormous soaring theme (as has often been remarked, one of the most striking features of Tippett's melodies is their sheer length) in a single, unbroken flow. It immediately proclaims Tippett as a composer of unusual power.

But it is in the finale that suddenly, and apparently out of nowhere, the style that is most closely associated with Tippett appears, fully-fledged. This movement is headed in the manuscript by a quotation from Blake: 'Damn braces, bless relaxes'. Here is its opening:

Ex. 2

This is an example of what is called additive rhythm. Instead of a
regular beat, as was the case with fast music up to the beginning of this
century, we have here an irregular alternation of patterns of two and
three (specifically, two quavers, three quavers and two crotchets).
The origins of this style are complex and hard to pin down precisely.
Undoubtedly Tippett had heard pieces by Stravinsky, who, though not
the first composer to make use of this kind of irregular rhythm, was the
first to use it extensively. But there is a fundamental difference between
Stravinsky's and Tippett's rhythmic languages. Compare this famous
passage from Stravinsky's *The Rite of Spring*, the opening of the final
'Sacrificial Dance', with the Tippett quoted above:

Ex. 3

In Tippett's Quartet the rhythm is dictated by the irregular contours
of the melody, and the melody is of primary importance; whereas in the
Stravinsky the rhythm is the overwhelmingly dominant feature (at the
end of the 'Sacrificial Dance' we feel that the rhythm is all). Closer in
spirit is the rhythmic technique of the English madrigal, of which
Tippett has a thorough knowledge, and whose direct influence on,
for example, the first movements of the Concerto for Double String
Orchestra and the Second String Quartet, is obvious. But the technique there is essentially one of independence of parts and irregularity
of phrases within a regular metre, with frequent use of tied notes

across the bar; whereas that of the First String Quartet's finale is the irregularity of the basic pulse. Perhaps we come closest to it in certain passages in folk-song. Unlike German folk-music, which is metrically rigid, British folk-music employs irregular rhythms (as does Russian folk-music, which is at the back of Stravinsky's additive technique). The melodies of British folk-song tend to follow the natural rhythm of the words rather than force them into a predetermined metrical pattern. Take, for example, the Welsh folk-song 'Lisa Lan', where the alternation of $\frac{2}{4}$ and $\frac{3}{4}$ bars gives the tune its graceful lilt:

Ex. 4

Tippett's additive technique cannot ultimately be traced back to any one particular source. We may suggest influences, but in the end we have to admit that what we encounter in the finale of the First Quartet is a musical language of remarkable originality.

Here, and in the outer, fast movements of the First Piano Sonata and the Concerto for Double String Orchestra, it is the rhythmic freedom of the music, its joyful liberation from orthodox notions of stress and phrase length, that contributes so much to its vitality. To pursue another analogy, there is a close correspondence between Tippett's use of additive rhythm and the 'sprung rhythm' of Gerard Manley Hopkins. Tippett's setting of Hopkins's sonnet 'The Wind-hover', which he made in 1942, perfectly matches the poem's rhythm and feeling. Here is the opening of Hopkins's poem:

I cáught this mórning mórning's mínion, kíng-
dom of dáylight's dáuphin, dapple-dáwn-drawn Fálcon, in his ríding
Of the rólling level úndernéath him steady aír, and stríding
Hígh there, how he rúng upon the réin of a wímpling wíng . . .

'In his ecstasy', the poem goes on; and in the attempt to capture the bird's ecstasy in poetry Hopkins makes use of all his extraordinary rhythmic technique and mastery of language. Though we have what is basically a five-stress line (and the first line, except that it ends with a half-word, is regular, giving the poem an orthodox start the better to show off its subsequent unorthodoxies), the proliferation of unstressed syllables in irregular groups between the stresses make the lines dance and spring, hence 'sprung rhythm'. There is a similar 'feel' to many of Tippett's melodies, and especially where he uses the same technique in music as Hopkins does in poetry, adding beats to, or subtracting them from, a basic metre to make the tune dance more exuberantly—a different kind of additive (or subtractive) technique to the First Quartet's—as in this tune from the last movement of the Concerto for Double String Orchestra:

Ex. 5

The language of this tune, with its joyful, winning lilt, is close to folk-song (compare the Welsh folk-song 'Lisa Lan' quoted above). The Concerto (1938–9), and its predecessor, the First Piano Sonata (1936–7), are full of such tunes and one feels Tippett is exulting in his new-found mastery. The Piano Sonata is more modest in scope than its companion and more restrained in its gaiety. Tippett at first called it 'Fantasy Sonata': the first movement is a set of variations and he felt that this disqualified it from genuine sonata status. In fact there are honourable classical precedents (such as Beethoven's op. 26), and the work's four well-contrasted movements, including a powerful scherzo, more than justify the title. The slow movement this time is based on a real folk tune, the Scottish song 'Ca' the Yowes'.

The Concerto for Double String Orchestra—'concerto' in the eighteenth-century sense of concerto grosso—is Tippett's first undoubted masterpiece and has become the most familiar and most frequently played of all his instrumental works. It brings to perfection the various lines of experiment tried out in the Quartet and the Sonata. The rhythmic language of the outer movements is of great subtlety, the polyphony smooth and effortless. The first movement is a sonata, though a lyrical rather than a dramatic one; without sharp contrasts, but with an even sense of movement, superbly sustained. The finale is a rondo, whose inspired second theme has already been quoted. The slow movement is based on another long and serenely beautiful tune for solo violin, the first eight bars of which are again modelled, rhythmically, on 'Ca' the Yowes'; while the middle section is the first published example of a Tippett fugue (though not a developed one), which establishes a continuity with Beethoven in its resemblance to the fugue in the slow movement of the op. 95 String Quartet. The richness of sound resulting from the use of a double string orchestra recalls another masterly precedent, Elgar's *Introduction and Allegro* for string quartet and string orchestra, which like Tippett's Concerto ends with a broad and sonorous statement of a folk-like tune. If Elgar here is on unfamiliar territory for him, Tippett is thoroughly at home: folk-song is now so much in his blood that he can write his own folk-like melodies without a hint of pastiche. His use of such melodies at this period is a deliberate 'popular' device—it goes with his socialism—and is much more natural and successful with him, because more deeply felt, than with most other composers who have been influenced by folk-song. It is indeed the unselfconsciousness of its language, combined with its formal mastery, that makes the Concerto for Double String Orchestra such a remarkable achievement.

CHAPTER FOUR

A Child of Our Time

It was against the background of his continuing involvement with left-wing politics that the culminating work of Tippett's first period took shape. In 1935 he joined the Communist Party, in common with other young idealists at that time; he did so, however, as a supporter of Trotsky, and hoped to convert his own branch of the Communist Party to the ideals which he identified with Trotsky. When, after a few months, he failed to do so, he left the party. He found in any case that he was too much of an individualist to be tied to a set of rigidly imposed dogmas. He realized that he had no useful role to play as a political activist; he was an artist, and the compassion he felt for the persecuted and oppressed, particularly those in Eastern Europe whose countries were being overrun by Hitler, people in the main overlooked by the radicals of the time (whose chief concern was the Spanish Civil War) as well as the establishment—this compassion could best be expressed by means of his art, in a musical work. Such a work began to grow inside him, at first in the form of an opera, on the Irish Easter Rebellion of 1916; then, because he realized he wanted a less dramatic and more contemplative form, an oratorio. In 1938 there came a crucial stimulus. 'When in November of that year', he has written, 'the cruellest and most deliberate of the Nazi pogroms was launched on the pretext of an incident in Paris, the personal amalgam of general compassion for all outcasts and particular susceptibility to the Nazi horror fused into a clear artistic image.' The incident in Paris was the shooting of a German diplomat, vom Rath, by a young Polish Jew, Grynszpan. The boy, the suffering outcast provoked into taking a tragic revenge, became the symbolic hero of *A Child of Our Time*.

Tippett asked T. S. Eliot, whom he had got to know well, and who was something of a father figure to him at that time, to write the libretto. Eliot agreed, but on condition that Tippett would first provide him with a detailed synopsis, including the number and the kinds of words he required for each section. When Tippett had done this, Eliot suggested that Tippett would do better to finish it himself, since anything that he, Eliot, might add, would be too obviously poetic. Eliot's advice was sound, and the finished libretto is all the better for being simple and direct. Tippett has said that he finds the most successful parts of the text to be those that most closely approach folk-idiom; for example, the solo tenor's:

> I have no money for my bread;
> I have no gift for my love.

For *A Child of Our Time* was intended as a popular work in the true sense of the word, in that it records and reflects the common experience of ordinary people rather than (though these are of course an integral part) Tippett's own personal experience and feelings.

In his search for the most appropriate musical forms for his words, Tippett turned to Bach and Handel. It is entirely characteristic of Tippett that to nourish his own work he should have drawn inspiration from masterpieces he loved. He is, in a real sense, a traditionalist. His relationship to the great composers of the past is a family one: it is natural for him to draw on their legacy. The three-part formal scheme of *A Child of Our Time* was consciously modelled on Handel's *Messiah*, while that work and the Bach Passions provided a model for the various types of music he employed: recitative, aria, dramatic chorus, congregational hymn. The last presented a major difficulty: what modern equivalent could Tippett find to Bach's Lutheran chorale, and what would evoke the same kind of common response? He did not want to use Christian hymns, for this would imply a specific commitment to Christianity, which he wished to avoid. For a long time the problem seemed insoluble. Then one day he heard a black singer on the radio sing the spiritual 'Steal Away'. 'At the phrase "The trumpet sounds within-a my soul" ', he has written, 'I was blessed with an immediate intuition: that I was being moved by this phrase in some way beyond what the musical phrase in itself warranted. I realized that in England or America everyone would be moved in this way, forcing me to see that the unique musical metaphor for this particular function in this particular oratorio had been found.' The spiritual, indeed, is a genuinely popular form and has a broadness of appeal that transcends any particular doctrine or faith. In *A Child of Our Time* Tippett used five spirituals, which occur at pivotal points of the work: the last, 'Deep River', provides its emotional climax. Here Tippett's framework of counterpoint effects the same kind of transformation of the original as did Bach's harmonizations of Lutheran chorales in the St. Matthew and St. John Passions (see Ex. 6 overleaf). The musical language of the work in general is never too far removed from the folk-idiom of the spirituals, so that they can always follow on quite naturally from what has gone before. It owes much to Tippett's own distillation of folk-song; there are also strong links with the nineteenth-century English oratorio tradition, stemming from Handel. But there is, too, as we might expect, much of the anguished chromaticism of our own time.

Out of the darkness of winter and the background of suffering and oppression with which the work begins comes the boy's act of defiance, which leads inevitably to his own death. Tippett presents the death of the boy not so much as a personal tragedy but as one inevitable event in a clash of dark forces, an event however out of which hope can begin to grow again. The idea of the boy's death as atonement is of course a powerful symbol, going back not only to Christianity but to the primitive religious concept of a necessary sacrifice at midwinter to bring back the departed sun. At the end of *A Child of Our Time* the predominant wintry imagery softens and the solo alto sings of the coming of spring. But, as Tippett makes clear, it is not in the scapegoat, the 'other', that the real solution to the problem of evil lies, but in ourselves. In the solo tenor's great line:

> I would know my shadow and my light,
> so shall I at last be whole

we have, in its essence, Tippett's fundamental conviction: that wisdom comes from the knowledge of one's own good and evil natures, and inner harmony from their reconciliation.

Tippett began work on the music of *A Child of Our Time* in September 1939, two days after the outbreak of the Second World War. It took him two years to write. Before the war began he had

B

Ex. 6

become a convinced pacifist, and in 1940 he joined the Peace Pledge Union, making its pledge, 'I renounce war and I will never support or sanction another', and registering as a conscientious objector. The Union had been founded in 1935 by the Reverend Dick Sheppard, and had attracted wide and enthusiastic support—its sponsors included Bertrand Russell and Aldous Huxley—although many of its original members had resigned at the beginning of the war. It is characteristic of Tippett that he should have joined the Union at its most difficult period. He has remained a pacifist ever since: he wrote a pamphlet, 'Abundance of Creation', for the Union in 1944; after the war he often spoke at its meetings; he became its Chairman in 1957 and its President in 1958.

The pacifist standpoint of *A Child of Our Time* is evident in such passages as the chorus's questions:

> Is the man of destiny master of us all?
> Shall those cast out be unavenged?

to which the solo bass replies:

> The man of destiny is cut off from fellowship.
> Healing springs from the womb of time.
> The simple-hearted shall exult in the end.

These were beliefs hard to hold on to in the face of such obvious evil as Nazism. The war was to try the strength of his convictions, and to prove them.

CHAPTER FIVE

The War: Morley College and Prison

When the Second World War broke out Tippett was thirty-four years old. He was still little known as a composer: the total of professional performances of his music was not yet into double figures and he had only completed two pieces to his satisfaction—the Piano Sonata and the Concerto for Double String Orchestra. However, Willy Strecker, the director of Schott's in Mainz, whom he had met in the interval of a concert performance of Hindemith's *Mathis der Maler* at the Queen's Hall and who had asked to see his music, had been sufficiently impressed by these two scores and the First String Quartet to write to London in August 1939 offering a publishing contract. But by the time the letter arrived the war had begun, and so actual publication of scores was delayed for several more years.

With the beginning of the war his work at Morley College expanded. In October 1940, shortly after a bomb had hit and severely damaged the main building so that classes had to be transferred to a neighbouring school, he was appointed Director of Music. Thus began a remarkable period for music at Morley. The college became a focal point for musical refugees from central Europe: among them the Hungarian composer and teacher Mátyás Seiber, Walter Bergmann (who was to collaborate with Tippett on editions of Purcell and his contemporaries), the string players who were later to form the Amadeus Quartet, and the conductor Walter Goehr. Concerts of early music became a speciality: the Elizabethan madrigalists, Purcell, Monteverdi, and the Bachs; they culminated in the first performance ever in Britain of the complete Monteverdi *Vespers*, which Tippett and Goehr edited and which Goehr conducted in 1946. There was modern music too and gifted young musicians to play it, including Peter Pears and Benjamin Britten, and the pianist and composer Noel

Mewton-Wood, who was tragically to take his own life at the age of thirty-one. The college choir was greatly increased in numbers and in capability: in 1943 they gave the first performance of Tippett's two madrigals *The Windhover* and *The Source*, written specially for them, and they later took part in the première of *A Child of Our Time*.

Tippett presided over all this activity with boundless enthusiasm, conducting the choir—though occasionally he would hand over to someone else and join in with his own fine tenor voice—giving informal lectures, inspiring everyone. And, in all the time he could spare, he composed. While writing *A Child of Our Time* he was also completing the *Fantasia on a Theme of Handel* for piano and orchestra which he had interrupted in 1939 in order to begin work on the oratorio. The latter part of the Fantasia was strongly influenced by the outbreak of the war and the new and more sombre world of *A Child of Our Time*: Tippett introduced the 'Dies Irae' theme and ended the work with a long and serious fugue. When he had finished *A Child of Our Time* he put the score to one side for a while and wrote his Second String Quartet. This piece shows an increasing mastery of his by now absolutely personal idiom. In the tortuous chromatic lines of the slow fugue that forms the second movement, and in the stern mood of much of the finale, we may feel a response to the immediate grimness of the world around him—this was the winter of 1941-2, one of the darkest periods of the war. Despite this, the first movement is an unbroken outpouring of joyful lyricism, while the scherzo is one of the most exuberant movements he was ever to write; and as well as being a *locus classicus* for additive rhythm it also provides a clear example of another technique very characteristic of Tippett, the extending of material by restatement in slightly altered form at a higher pitch. The finale is closely modelled on the last movement of Beethoven's C sharp minor Quartet, op. 131, and shows mastery of classical form and tonality. The Second Quartet was the first piece of Tippett's to be recorded commercially.

John Amis, who was then one of a number of young music-student and composer friends, has described how Tippett lived at that time in his Oxted cottage:

Michael's day would begin with the sound of grinding coffee beans. After breakfast, he would shut himself up in the living-room and then a noise would ensue of singing, groaning, shrieking, laughing, a curious declaimed humming and much piano banging. . . . Weekday lunch would be cooked by someone from the farm on whose fringe the cottage stood, and then came a walk during which wood was collected for the fire and ideas sifted for whatever composition was in hand. . . . Home for tea, more work—copying maybe, although mostly he used to compose straight on to full score—then supper, prepared by Michael, if possible something 'off the estate', for he has always liked to live off the land. After supper, books and bed; but if friends were there—most welcome at the week-end, firmly despatched first thing Monday morning, for Michael quickly got fractious if not allowed to work—there might be a record or two, Stravinsky, the Boulanger Monteverdi set, but more likely Bessie Smith or some wild spirituals; and then a spate of talk. Michael was so generous with ideas with young people, so gay about his own problems, so gentle and perceptive about ours. Last thing at night we might ask Michael what his composition score was that day: the average was about three or four bars!

Tippett had met Peter Pears and Benjamin Britten shortly after they returned from the United States in 1942 and they asked him to write a piece for them. The eventual result was the cantata for voice and piano *Boyhood's End*, on a text by the naturalist W. H. Hudson. Tippett chose a passage from the chapter in Hudson's autobiography where he describes how at the age of fifteen he began to be afraid that he might lose that peculiarly close contact and kinship with nature that he had had as a boy on the great plains of Argentina. The words that open the cantata are a statement of his predicament (see Ex. 7). In fact Hudson never did lose his delight in nature; and the radiant gaiety of the music here and elsewhere in the work makes it clear that Tippett too had 'kept what he had'.

In the autumn of 1943 he was summoned to appear before a tribunal to justify his conscientious objection to war service. Despite the valuable work he was doing at Morley, not to speak of his work as a composer, he was not given absolute exemption. Various non-combatant jobs were suggested and eventually he was directed into full-time farm work. But he felt that he must make a stand on the importance *he* assigned to his music, and consequently he deliberately

Ex. 7

failed to comply with the directions. He was brought to trial at Oxted Magistrates' Court and sentenced to three months' imprisonment. Vaughan Williams spoke in his defence, describing his compositions as 'a distinct national asset' and his teaching at Morley as 'work of national importance'; but the magistrate did not agree.

He served his sentence in Wormwood Scrubs. He was not entirely cut off from music: he took over the prison orchestra. Its previous conductor, he was amused to discover, had been Ivor Novello. Prison was in no sense an embittering experience, on the contrary, it was a very positive one; it was the necessary test of his beliefs, and it seemed absolutely right, for himself and his music, that he should have had to go through with it.

When he came out of prison he resumed his work at Morley. It was about this time that Britten, who had been impressed by what he knew of Tippett's music, asked him whether he had written any large-scale pieces. Tippett showed him the score of *A Child of Our Time*: Britten was enthusiastic and encouraged him to try to arrange a performance. The various difficulties of producing a big choral work under wartime conditions were eventually surmounted, and *A Child of Our Time* was performed at the Adelphi Theatre on 19 March 1944. Peter Pears was the tenor soloist and Walter Goehr conducted. It was a landmark in Tippett's career. *The Times* wrote:

> Tippett has succeeded to a quite remarkable extent in creating a powerful work out of a contemplation of the evil abroad in the world of yesterday and today. Perhaps because he has written his own text in terse, pregnant sentences he has succeeded in combining the force of the particular with the significance of the universal.

Slowly, but inevitably, he was beginning to be recognized.

Tippett's next undertaking was his most ambitious orchestral piece so far: the First Symphony. The symphony is a form that has presented peculiar difficulties to the contemporary composer: it is here that the examples of the classical masters, Haydn, Mozart and Beethoven, and their Romantic successors, Schubert, Brahms, Bruckner and Mahler, have cast their most inhibiting shadows. It is perhaps because of Tippett's peculiarly close involvement with Beethoven that he has undauntedly chosen to write in each of the three media that Beethoven made especially his own: piano sonata, string quartet and symphony. But, more precisely, it was his preoccupation in the early 1940s with writing tonal music of the Beethovenian dynamic kind, using and extending Beethoven's type of sonata form (most notably in the first movement of the First String Quartet and the finale of the Second), that led him inevitably to the symphony.

As has been noted, he wrote a symphony in the mid 1930s which did not satisfy him. By 1945, when he wrote his definitive First Symphony, he had acquired the technique to deal with those problems he had been unable to solve ten years before. The Concerto for Double String Orchestra and the two string quartets had proved his ability to write extended sonata movements, maintaining the old tonal tensions but making them sound fresh; now he had also to write a dense contrapuntal texture for full orchestra, with which it is a much more difficult task to achieve a proper balance than with the string quartet or string orchestra. The Symphony's first movement, the largest he had so far attempted, is a complete artistic success; it moves forward with unhalting vigour, sometimes breaking out characteristically into lyricism, as in this passage for the strings from the close of the exposition:

Ex. 8

There is no doubt that, given a good performance, this movement does come off, but in fact the First Symphony has probably suffered more in the past from poor performances than any other of Tippett's compositions: unless the complex rhythms and long phrases are articulated with absolute effortlessness, the music will not dance, but hobble. It is a characteristic of Tippett's music, as it is of Beethoven's, that poor performances make it sound exaggeratedly clumsy. This especially applies to his orchestral music; and since nearly every orchestral work of Tippett's has begun life with a less than first-rate performance, it is easy to understand why in the past he has been criticized for awkwardness and lack of clarity. It has invariably taken about ten years for orchestras to become sufficiently familiar with a new Tippett piece to play it confidently and well.

The second movement's variations over a ground bass stem, as Tippett acknowledges, from his love of Purcell. This movement, which alternates dark, brooding music with grimly passionate outbursts, is a deeply felt response to the suffering of the war, and a culmination of the kind of compassionate yet objective music that had found expression throughout *A Child of Our Time*, and in the slow movement of the Second String Quartet. The scherzo has a still earlier model, for the idea of a fast movement in triple time which keeps 'taking off' into groups of four in the time of three was derived from similar practice in the music of the medieval French master Pérotin. It has a soaring madrigal-like trio for strings. The finale is a big double fugue and is Tippett's most audacious attempt to unite the fugue with the sonata, as Beethoven had done in the last movement of the 'Hammerklavier' sonata and elsewhere. All Tippett's fugues are Beethovenian rather than Bachian fugues; that is to say, they are sonata-related, and dynamic rather than static. Their originality lies in Tippett's individual fusion of dynamism and lyricism. Here the first fugue is dynamic, the second lyrical. The movement's climax, after the two fugues have combined, is unexpectedly broken apart by repeated bass Es, underlined by timpani and bass drum. Fragments of the fugues are scattered to the winds and the Symphony ends with a quiet, sustained E (the dominant of the Symphony's home key of A major) on cellos and basses, full of expectation.

The preoccupation with fugue was carried over into the next work, the Third String Quartet, which contains no less than three fugal movements. The serene confidence of the first movement's opening chords, prefacing the first and most highly wrought of the fugues, might be compared—by no means to Tippett's detriment—with the opening of Beethoven's E flat Quartet, op. 127:

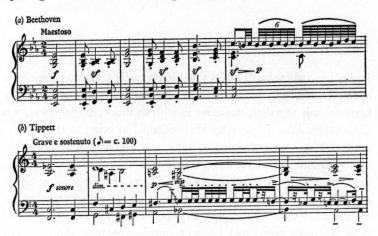

Ex. 9

Of Tippett's two contrasting slow movements, placed second and fourth, the one is a sustained outpouring of song-like counterpoint; the other an extraordinary thrice-repeated crescendo: from a single, long-held note, other notes grow, proliferate, intensify and eventually flood over into passionate lyricism. Such music demonstrates the inadequacy—the futility, even—of any attempts at verbal description, although at the same time it seems to invite it.

CHAPTER SIX

The Midsummer Marriage

It was inevitable that Tippett should eventually come to compose an opera. Opera, which, when all its disparate elements are working harmoniously together, can move us with an almost magic power, was the ideal medium for a composer concerned to bring us through his art to a deeper understanding of ourselves. The idea of an opera had long been contemplated and prepared for: he had gained much practical experience with his ballad operas *Robin Hood* and *The Village Opera* and the two children's operas that he wrote (or rather arranged) in collaboration with Christopher Fry in the late 1930s. At the same time, as already mentioned, he had planned an opera on the subject of the 1916 Easter Rebellion. Now a very different kind of work sprang into his imagination: a modern comedy, in which everyday events were to be set in a mythological and symbolic context.

In each of Tippett's operas we shall have to deal to some extent with the background, both musical and literary, to which the work is related and out of which it grows. We have already noticed the shaping influence of the Bach Passions and Handel's *Messiah* on *A Child of Our Time*. In *The Midsummer Marriage* the literary background in particular is rather complicated. The verse plays of Eliot and Auden, and Shaw's *Getting Married*, should at least be mentioned; but the work which provides the clearest key to the elucidation of the opera is Shakespeare's *A Midsummer Night's Dream*. The basic dramatic idea of *A Midsummer Night's Dream*, the interaction between the natural and supernatural words (in Shakespeare, the world of the fairies) and the resolution by supernatural means of the complications attending two pairs of lovers, is also that of *The Midsummer Marriage*. As for the musical background, the chief source-work is Mozart's *The Magic Flute*: there are intentional parallels between Mark and Jenifer in

Tippett's opera and Tamino and Pamina in Mozart's, and between Jack and Bella and Papageno and Papagena; and the idea of trials, so important to Tippett's conception, is also derived from *The Magic Flute*.

The immediate inspiration for *The Midsummer Marriage* can be traced to an event as specific as the one that set in motion *A Child of Our Time*. It is related very clearly to Tippett's interest in the psychology of Jung, and something should first be said about this, as the opera is difficult to explain without reference to Jungian terminology. I can only touch on a few of Jung's ideas here: the first and perhaps most important is that there is a level of the mind to which we may gain access in our dreams, that lies beyond, or perhaps more accurately below, our own personalities. Jung noticed that the same myths and religious ideas are common to different cultures, and came to the conclusion that the source of myth and religion is an unconscious world, existing in the sub-personal area of the mind, which is shared by all human beings. He called this the collective unconscious. The symbolic figures and signs which dwell in the collective unconscious Jung called archetypes. An archetype can be a mythical figure like a hero or a goddess; it can be a religious idea, like the cross of Christianity; or it can be an image of some basic experience, like that of the opposite sex. Jung called a man's archetypal image of woman the anima, and a woman's archetypal image of man the animus. (Anima and animus have a wide range of meaning for Jung: the anima is also the feminine side of man, and the animus the masculine side of woman.) The archetypes we meet in dreams may have immense significance for us, if we know how to interpret them. They may help us towards a spiritual maturity, a wholeness, which Jung regarded as the true end of life: the process by which this wholeness may be achieved he called 'individuation'—truly becoming oneself.

Tippett found himself in considerable sympathy with Jung's ideas; and the process of individuation as described by Jung was something he felt he must himself undertake. As we have seen, *A Child of Our Time* is preoccupied with the search for wholeness, which is identified in that work with man's acceptance of his dark self or his 'shadow' (the unconscious unknown part of the self, another important Jungian archetype). It was during the composition of *A Child of Our Time* that

Tippett himself underwent a short period of analysis from the English Jungian John Layard, and afterwards continued his own self-analysis.

There is an essay by Jung in which he distinguishes two types of art which he calls psychological and visionary: the former is concerned with experiences on a purely human level; the latter deals with the unfamiliar and strange. 'It can be a revelation whose heights or depths are beyond our fathoming, or a vision of beauty which we can never put into words. This disturbing spectacle of some tremendous process that in every way transcends our human feeling and understanding makes quite other demands upon the powers of the artist than do the experiences of the foreground of life.' Clearly these two types of art are the products of two fundamentally different kinds of temperament: one might legitimately call them Freudian (psychological) and Jungian (visionary). Jung's theory is concerned essentially with literature, but it can be extended quite naturally to the other arts. In painting, William Blake is an obvious example of a 'visionary' artist; whereas someone like Hogarth is clearly at the opposite extreme, a 'psychological' artist through and through. With music we are on trickier ground, since it might be argued that it is by its nature a visionary art; however, the distinction can certainly be made. Richard Strauss is a 'psychological' composer, for instance; whereas Tippett is unequivocally one of Jung's visionaries, and indeed the first inspiration for *The Midsummer Marriage* (a visual rather than a musical one) came in the form of just such a revelation as Jung describes. Tippett saw 'a stage picture of a wooded hilltop with a temple, where a warm and soft young man was being rebuffed by a cold and hard young woman . . . to such a degree that the collective, magical archetypes take charge—Jung's *anima* and *animus*: the girl, inflated by the latter, rises through the stage-flies to heaven, and the man, overwhelmed by the former, descends through the stage floor to hell. But it was clear that they would soon return. For I saw the girl later descending in a costume reminiscent of the goddess Athena . . . and the man ascending in one reminiscent of the god Dionysus.'

Out of this initial vision there came eventually an opera about the marriage at midsummer (the year's climax) of two young couples. The first, Mark and Jenifer, the pair of the vision, are complex and exalted; but at the beginning of the opera they are still in a state of spiritual innocence or unawareness, and before they can be married it is necessary for them to be parted and to undergo ordeals, or rather processes of transformation (which, as in the initial vision, are shown on the stage symbolically as ascents and descents), during which they discover deeper levels of themselves than they were previously aware of. Mark must discover and recognize the feminine part of himself (his anima), Jenifer the masculine part of herself (her animus): once again, as in *A Child of Our Time*, Tippett puts forward Jung's basic idea of the reconciliation of opposites as the necessary way to maturity and wholeness. In a sense Mark and Jenifer stand for all of us: all, that is, who feel compelled towards self-knowledge. The Chorus recognize this as they sing:

> Let Mark and Jenifer endure for us
> The perils of the royal way.

The second couple—Jack, a mechanic, and Bella, a secretary—are a much more straightforward and earthly pair whose marriage can therefore be celebrated without complication, though Jack achieves his own maturity in Act Three when he refuses to obey King Fisher's command to shoot at Sosostris and thus (we feel) wins the right to marry Bella. When—in the Ritual Dances in Act Two—they are presented with a symbolic enaction of their coming together, they fail to understand what is going on: this is Mark and Jenifer's world. These three dances, in which female animals (hound, otter and hawk) are shown hunting males (hare, fish and bird) are also associated with three elements: earth, water, air; and three seasons: autumn, winter, spring. At the climax of Act Three, a culminating fourth dance, 'Fire in Summer', symbolic of rebirth and creative love, is performed before Mark and Jenifer and the Chorus. (The set of four Ritual Dances, extracted from the opera in the form of a symphonic suite, has become one of Tippett's best-known pieces of music.)

The mythic world of transformation to which Mark and Jenifer gain access is guarded by the Ancients, who are priest and priestess of the temple around which the action takes place. They are in part modelled on Shaw's Ancients in *Back to Methuselah*, who in that play are personifications of mature wisdom. In total opposition to this world we have the proud, ruthless businessman King Fisher, who is Jenifer's father and Bella's employer. His name both evokes his worldly success (Tippett says that it is meant to be the same kind of name as Duke Ellington) and also brings to mind the Fisher King of the Grail legends, whose wound must be healed before his waste land becomes fertile again, though the connection is rather distant. King Fisher opposes the marriage, and fails to understand what Jenifer's and Mark's quest means: he tries first, unsuccessfully, to storm the Ancients' domain by force and then to use a clairvoyante, Sosostris (her name is taken from Eliot's *The Waste Land*, a further device of resonance), to discover what is happening. But he cannot face the truth—Jenifer united with Mark—when he sees it, and must die: his death is not only the inevitable result of his actions (he attempts to shoot Mark, but falls dead at his glance) but is obviously 'right' symbolically. It precipitates the fourth Ritual Dance, of rebirth.

Tippett wrote his own libretto. He had come to realize that in writing an opera, for him, as for Wagner, words and music, the dramatic scheme and its setting, are all essential parts of the creative act, and must all be his responsibility. The experience of *A Child of Our Time*, too, had increased his confidence. The composition of the music cost him six years of arduous work, from 1946 until 1952; yet what immediately strikes us about the music of *The Midsummer Marriage* is its spontaneity, the way it surges forward with apparent effortlessness. Each of the many sorts of musical language that Tippett now had at his command is strongly represented. There are passages of the purest lyricism, as for example Mark's first aria—sung in the full joy of his innocent young love, before Jenifer's rebuff sets in motion the necessary ordeals (Ex. 10). Then there is the kind of dynamic allegro music, as at the beginning and end of Act One, which Tippett has inherited from Beethoven. He is perhaps the only composer born in this century to whom this kind of expression has come quite naturally; it is essentially an unforced utterance springing from spontaneous abundance of vitality. Akin to it—when the music needs to dance rather than to run—is his additive scherzo style, which we find here elaborately developed in the Ritual Dances. The choral writing —of which there is a great deal, since the Chorus, as commentators on the action, play as important a part in *The Midsummer Marriage* as in Greek drama—is often of a similar exuberance and brightness (as

Ex. 10

opposed to the mostly dark, reflective writing in *A Child of Our Time*).
It shows the extent of Tippett's inheritance from the English madrigalists and from Purcell; for some of the writing (like the off-stage
chorus at the beginning of Act Two) is a superb recreation of seven-
teenth-century choral style. The vocal writing in general owes much
to Purcell, whereas *A Child of Our Time* largely followed on from
Tippett's immediate predecessors in the English oratorio tradition.
Britten had independently recreated a Purcellian style in his own way:
as an earlier generation of English composers had gone back to the

Elizabethans, so Tippett and Britten of all their predecessors found in Purcell the closest spirit.

Lastly, there is the kind of music perhaps most especially associated with *The Midsummer Marriage*: the 'magic' music which occurs at those moments in the drama when the two worlds of reality and myth coalesce. Ex. 11 shows a characteristic example of such music, the moment towards the end of Act One when Jenifer returns to the stage from 'heaven', and relates her experiences there. This kind of ecstatic music is always liable to overflow into burgeoning demisemiquavers, as if the rapture could not be contained. (The fourth movement of the Third String Quartet was such a place.) It is a type of expression that plays an increasingly large part in Tippett's mature music.

The music of *The Midsummer Marriage* as a whole, intensely joyful, optimistic, life-affirming, is quite contrary to the spirit of the time,* for this was just after the end of the Second World War, after the concentration camps had been opened and the full, unspeakable horror of Nazism revealed; after the first atomic bombs had been dropped on Hiroshima and Nagasaki and inaugurated our present Age of Anxiety, as Auden called it. Much post-war art has tended to reflect a sense of exhaustion and hopelessness, either by retreating into a narrow hermetic world or by more overt gestures of despair; yet Tippett, who was as aware as anyone of the suffering in the world, was able to stand apart from it and deal in a superbly positive way with the problems of self-knowledge, which are, perhaps, the most urgent of all, if the world is not to be destroyed. In 1938 he had written: 'An artist can certainly be in opposition to the external "spirit of the age" and in tune with some inner need, as, for instance, Blake was. A composer's intuitions of what his age is really searching for may be, and probably will be, not in the least such obvious things as the portrayal

---

* On the other hand I am aware that *The Midsummer Marriage* can also be seen as part of a neo-romantic movement which flourished in this country immediately after the Second World War—including the poetry of Dylan Thomas, the plays of Christopher Fry, the paintings and poetry of David Jones, and works of Britten such as the *Spring Symphony*—and whose optimism is a true reflection of one aspect of the 'spirit of the time': the tremendous sense of liberation after the war and the confidence that society could be rebuilt and transformed.

Ex. 11

of stress and uncertainty by grim and acid harmonies. The important thing . . . is that he should be in some living contact with the age.'

The Midsummer Marriage was accepted for performance at Covent

Garden and first performed there on 27 January 1955. Many of the critics were baffled by the strangeness of the work, and what appeared to them to be a mystifying and over-complex libretto, though most of them sensed the quality of the music. Barbara Hepworth's designs, even if artistically outstanding, may have tended to obscure rather than elucidate the action. Time was needed before the opera's apparent difficulties became clear. For the music, Norman Del Mar's superb 1963 BBC studio performance was the turning-point, followed by the 1968 Covent Garden revival conducted by Colin Davis, which was later recorded. But the Welsh National Opera production of 1976 has been the most successful so far in conveying on stage the true spirit of this rich and complex work, which almost everyone now recognizes for the masterpiece that it is.

CHAPTER SEVEN

Four Major Works

The biography of the mature composer since the war is uneventful; it becomes more and more the history of his music. During the composition of *The Midsummer Marriage* there had been a few significant changes in Tippett's life. At the end of 1950 he moved from his cottage at Oxted to Tidebrook Manor, near Wadhurst in Sussex, a large, somewhat dilapidated house on a hillside overlooking a broad sweep of the Weald. He shared this house with his mother, who was now a widow and in her seventies.

In June 1951, after conducting a series of concerts for the Festival of Britain, he retired as Director of Music from Morley College in order to be able to devote most of his time to composition. He had begun to give broadcast talks for the BBC after the war and found that they provided a useful small secondary income. Some of these talks and other writings were later published as a book, *Moving into Aquarius*, which is an excellent introduction to his ideas, both musical and philosophical.

In the wake of *The Midsummer Marriage* came four masterly works, which to a certain extent draw on the language of the opera, and especially on the magical world of its Second Act. (The direct influence of *The Midsummer Marriage* persisted for at least five years after its completion, and can be felt in small-scale works such as the Sonata for Four Horns of 1955 as well as in the major pieces.) Stylistically, Tippett's slow music now tends to become more ornamented, the polyphony denser, and the individual lines more melismatic, in order to express an increasingly ecstatic vision; while the fast music, developing on from the Ritual Dances, becomes rougher and more boisterous. Tippett's motto for *The Midsummer Marriage*, which he set at the head of the score, was 'You shall say: I am a child of earth and of starry heaven'. Particularly in the two big orchestral works from this period we feel this polarity: the slow music (as, for instance, the slow movement of the Piano Concerto) aspiring towards heaven, and the fast music (like the first movement of the Second Symphony) firmly rooted in the earth, while the single full-scale scherzo movement from the period, the one in the Second Symphony, dances between the two spheres.

The first of these four works is the song-cycle *The Heart's Assurance* for high voice and piano, written for Peter Pears in 1951 before *The Midsummer Marriage* was finished. Tippett set three poems by Alun Lewis and two by Sidney Keyes, both men being outstandingly gifted poets who were killed in the Second World War, Lewis at twenty-eight, Keyes at only twenty. The songs are all strophic, which is to say that the poems are written in verses and the music follows the verse shape. In writing strophic songs Tippett was placing himself in the tradition of, among many others, Schubert, another composer for whom he feels a close affinity. Tippett has remarked of Schubert's songs that often the poetry he sets is poor, but this does not affect the quality of the song. In the case of *The Heart's Assurance* the poems are good ones; but when a poem is set to music, Tippett says, one is no longer able, nor is there any need, to appreciate it as poetry: 'The music of a song destroys the verbal music of a poem utterly. I am inclined to think that a composer responds less to a poem's verbal sound, when he chooses that poem as a vehicle for his musical art, than to the poem's situation, lyrical or dramatic.' This is a rather contentious statement: as Peter Pears has remarked, one might more truly speak of the relationship between music and poem as a happy marriage than of one destroying the other—but it obviously reflects what Tippett felt to be the truth about his own song-cycle, at the time he wrote it. What is clear is that the situation, the common theme of the five poems, which is love under the shadow of death, was for him the most important factor, over and above the individual words of the poems. If we respond to the refrain of the last poem: 'Young men ... Remember your lovers', it is because, Tippett would have it, we are responding to the general situation of the poem; we are not responding to the words as poetry. Whatever the truth of this—and it is hard to accept that we are not also responding in some measure to the poetry in the words—we have in

Tippett's setting a superb fusion of words and music, and which is especially moving when the refrain appears for the fourth and last time at the very end of the song, and the cycle:

Ex. 12

The Heart's Assurance is an intensely personal work, being dedicated to Francesca Allinson, a woman whom Tippett had loved, and who, in 1945, committed suicide. Nevertheless, Tippett has said, 'I was able to discharge my personal emotion into the general poetic expression, and to select from two poets . . . the poems that gave me an artistically satisfactory series of poems for songs. . . . To hammer home my chief point about song as an art form, I need only state that when we listen to this song-cycle based on the work of two poets, we are completely unaware of which poet is which.'

The work which stands closest to *The Midsummer Marriage* in its language and its sustained lyrical flow is the Piano Concerto of 1953–5. This began, like the two other orchestral works to be considered here, with the stimulus of a musical experience from another piece, in this case Beethoven's Fourth Piano Concerto, whose first movement Tippett had heard Walter Gieseking play at a rehearsal in 1950 for a concert in which his own First Symphony was also being performed. 'Under the influence of an exceptionally poetic yet classical perform-ance of the Beethoven movement, I found myself persuaded that a contemporary concerto might be written, in which the piano is used once again for its poetic capabilities.' The majority of successful twentieth-century piano concertos—there are not many; one thinks immediately of the three by Bartók, then one pauses to think again— have tended to emphasize the piano's percussive qualities: this is especially true of Bartók's first two concertos which are the master-pieces of this particular manner. Tippett on the other hand is con-cerned to make the piano sing, which it does right from the opening bars (see Ex. 13). This opening (which provides a classic example of Tippett's use of harmony based on the interval of a fourth, a technique he derived from Hindemith but which he has made especially his own) is a sustained crescendo, thirty-three bars long, leading to a sonorous tutti. The effect is similar to the opening of Act Two of *The Mid-summer Marriage* and there is a similar feeling of exultation at the climax: a joyful opening-out. What this climax and others later do not offer is a chance for the pianist to show off in bravura passages; nor, though at times the sound of the orchestra recalls nineteenth-century predecessors—Brahms more than Beethoven—is there any sense of a dramatic conflict between soloist and orchestra, the one trying to assert its superiority over the other. There is plenty of dialogue, some of it very lively, as, most notably, in the passage towards the end of the slow movement where the violins and violas, entering for the first time in

Ex. 13

the movement, rush about in fervid demisemiquavers and resist for some time the repeated attempts of the piano to calm them. But for most of the concerto, soloist and orchestra are on genial terms. The closeness of the relationship is emphasized by the ingenious idea of including a celesta (a familiar voice from *The Midsummer Marriage*)

in the orchestra and letting it join the piano in the latter's first movement cadenza. The intermingling of their sounds, the one like a
muted echo of the other, is magical.

With the *Fantasia Concertante on a Theme of Corelli* the inspirational
piece is actually present in the score. Tippett, asked by the Edinburgh
Festival to provide a work for the three-hundredth anniversary of
Corelli's birth in 1953, decided he would take a piece by Corelli and
build a composition around it. He chose an Adagio in F minor with a
short vivace postscript in C major; highly appropriate for him as it
expresses both the dark and light sides of Corelli's personality. Corelli's
theme begins the piece and the ensuing variations gradually move over
from Corelli's world into Tippett's. Eventually we reach a fugue—
which at its start incorporates a short passage from Bach's organ fugue
on a theme of Corelli—and a long, slow ascent from darkness into light.
Its radiant climax and the quiet Pastorale that follows (quoted in
Ex. 1) are among Tippett's most inspired pages. This work is Tippett's
mature complement to the Concerto for Double String Orchestra; it
is the more complex statement of a composer who in the fifteen years
since the Concerto had gained much in wisdom but lost nothing of
his gift of lyric spontaneity.

The culminating masterpiece of this period, which also points the
way towards the next, is the Second Symphony of 1956–7. Returning
to the symphony after more than ten years, Tippett came up with a
fresh set of answers to its special problems. The obsession with
Beethovenian dynamism is still evident, particularly in the first
movement, one of his most successful re-formations of the sonata
allegro. The solution proposed here is a neoclassical one, which
results partly from the influence of Stravinsky's neoclassical works,
notably his two symphonies, and partly from the direct inspiration of a
Vivaldi concerto which, as Tippett has described, he heard on tape
while looking out over the sunlit Lake Lugano, and whose pounding
bass Cs 'suddenly threw me from Vivaldi's world into my own'.
Tippett's first movement begins with these pounding bass Cs, and the
complex figurations built up over them and other long-sustained pedals
have an eighteenth-century feeling and an eighteenth-century strength:
the often clashing polytonal harmony of the upper parts does nothing
to undermine the stability of the bass. At the end of the movement

trumpets and timpani hammer home the Cs with rock-like firmness in an unequivocal C major.

Tippett planned the four movements—the Symphony has the traditional four-movement scheme of sonata allegro, slow movement, scherzo and finale—as, broadly speaking, expressive of four emotional states: joy, tenderness, gaiety, fantasy; and the different and varied sorts of music within each movement correspond to these general headings. Thus in the first movement we have the exuberant, active, masculine joy of the opening—this is music of the earth indeed:

Ex. 14

contrasted with the more restrained and lyrical, passive, feminine joy of the second subject:

Ex. 15

The first dances, the second sings.

At the start of the slow movement a soft trumpet call accompanied by piano and harp announces another slow, magical ascent for the cellos. This music, abruptly cut off by a trumpet fanfare, with pizzicato strings and sharp chords for wind and piano whose spiky sound is a foretaste of the future, is succeeded by a wonderfully tender passage for the strings, as full of human warmth as the first was full of natural serenity:

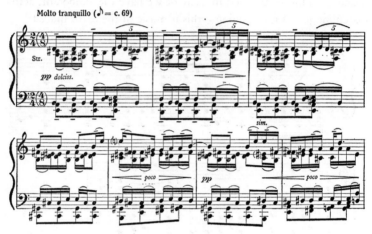

Ex. 16

The two kinds of music alternate, but the human music becomes shorter each time until, to quote Wilfrid Mellers, 'it dissolves into the angelic voices of birds and rustling leaves'. The scherzo, a dance first for the woodwind and then for the strings, is in Tippett's most sophisticated additive manner. Its boisterous middle section provokes a Dionysiac outburst for the full orchestra, with antiphonal trumpets. The finale begins with sounds which strongly anticipate *King Priam*. It is in the form of a Fantasia, with four unrelated sections. The short introduction generates a lively set of variations over a ground: the strident brass music, a new sound here, will become a familiar Tippett fingerprint in the music of the 1960s. The third section is an enormously long *cantabile* melody which gradually descends in two broad paragraphs from a high A flat down five and a half octaves until it reaches the low C of the Symphony's opening; whereupon the pounding Cs start up again for what Tippett calls 'five gestures of farewell'. In the last of these the solo trumpet's final descent to a sonorous middle C over a C-based sustained chord (the same chord as at bar 7 of Ex. 14) is one of the securest sounds in twentieth-century music.

CHAPTER EIGHT

King Priam

In 1957 Tippett was asked by the Koussevitsky Foundation to write a piece for chorus and orchestra. He accepted the commission, but when he began to think about it seriously he found his thoughts turning inexorably towards another opera, and the Foundation generously extended their commission to allow him to write one. *King Priam* took him three years to complete, half the time he had needed for *The Midsummer Marriage*; but the difficult experience of the first opera made the composition of the second less problematic, and the score itself was far less complex and employed a smaller apparatus. Once again he was his own librettist.

The opera was first performed at the Coventry Festival in 1962 celebrating the opening of the new cathedral, which had been built on the foundations of the medieval one destroyed by bombs in the Second World War. The theme of the festival was peace. Both *King Priam* and the other major work given its première there, Britten's *War Requiem*, dealt with 'war, and the pity of war'—Wilfred Owen's words, which stand at the head of Britten's score—and both treated of the possible reconciliation, difficult though this is in our time, which might come out of the suffering that war engenders.

That Tippett's second opera is totally different from his first should cause no surprise. Tippett is not the sort of composer who, once he has thoroughly explored a particular world, is content to stay in its comfortable surroundings; he is driven on to discover new ground. And, as we have seen, an important element in his art is contrast, the juxtaposition of opposites. Whereas *The Midsummer Marriage* was lyrical, expansive, and a comedy in the broad sense that all comes right in the end, *King Priam* is a taut, stark tragedy, as hard and compact as the other was prolific as a growing tree. This is not to say that there

Tippett, right, with his mother and brother, *c.* 1908

The sitting room in Tippett's parents' house at Wetherden, Suffolk, where he lived from 1905 until 1919

PROGRAMME.

Concerto in D for Flutes, Oboe, Horns and Strings.

Allegro non troppo.   Andante espressivo.   Allegro scherzando

Allegro non troppo

Three Songs.

1. Afternoon Tea.   2. Sea Love.   3. Arracombe Wood.

Soloist - ERIC SHAXSON.   Accompanist - DORA MILNER.

"Jockey to the Fair."

Piano Solo.   LESLIE ORRIE, A.R.C.M.

Grotrian-Steinweg Piano.

INTERVAL.

String Quartet in F.

Allegro con brio.   Andante Expressivo.

Adagio non troppo, con molto sentimento.

Allegro non troppo, molto leggiero.

Allegro con brio.

JOHN MORLEY.   HELEN STEWART

MAURICE HARDY.   MARY GLADDEN.

Psalm in C for Chorus and Orchestra.

Conductor: DAVID EVANS, Mus. Bac.

Left,
the programme of a concert at the Barn Theatre, Oxted, in April 1930 (see p. 22). Although no composer's name appeared, all the items were in fact by Tippett. The conductor, David Moule Evans, was a fellow student at the Royal College of Music

Below, the Barn Theatre as it is today

Right, Tippett at a rehearsal of *A Child of Our Time* in February 1945

Below, the composer with Yehudi Menuhin at a rehearsal of the *Fantasia Concertante on a Theme of Corelli* in 1966

The first page of the manuscript of the Concerto for Double String
Orchestra, 1938

The first page of the manuscript of the Fourth Symphony, 1976

Première of *The Midsummer Marriage* at the Royal Opera House, Covent Garden, in 1955, produced by Christopher West, with scenery by Barbara Hepworth and choreography by John Cranko. Joan Sutherland as Jenifer, Richard Lewis as Mark, in Act Three

King Priam, Act Two. The first production, 1962, by Sam Wanamaker, with designs by Sean Kenny. Left to right: John Dobson as Paris, Victor Godfrey as Hector

The Knot Garden, Act Three. The American première at the School of Music, Northwestern University, 1974. Craig Pollock as Faber-Ferdinand

The Ice Break, Act One. The American première, 1979, by the Opera Company of Boston, directed by Sarah Caldwell, with (left to right) Leigh Munro as Gayle, Jake Gardner as Yuri, and Cynthia Clarey as Hannah

is no continuity between the two operas. Indeed, in a sense *King Priam* follows on quite naturally from *The Midsummer Marriage*. It begins with Priam and Hecuba as a young couple, and there is a tableau, 'Priam and Hecuba go out as the royal pair', which may remind us strongly of Mark and Jenifer. *The Midsummer Marriage* was concerned with personal development, with how particularly the 'royal pair' Mark and Jenifer reach a state of maturity at which they may come together as man and wife. *King Priam* takes us out of the personal life into the world, into history; and on one level at least the facts of history have been essentially tragic.

The legend of the Trojan War, as found in Homer's *Iliad*, is one of the oldest in Western culture. Homer tells the story from the Greek side: Tippett, like Virgil in *The Aeneid*, chooses to tell it from the Trojan side. At the start of the opera, Priam, king of Troy, and Hecuba his wife are warned by a soothsayer that their infant son Paris will cause the death of his father. Priam orders that the child be killed, but the guard gives him instead to a shepherd to be brought up. Years later Priam meets the boy Paris, recognizes him and accepts him back into Troy as his son. Paris goes to the court of King Menelaus of Sparta, falls in love with Menelaus' wife Helen and abducts her to Troy. On this pretext the Trojan War begins; the Greeks besiege Troy. Achilles, greatest of the Greek heroes, will not fight because the Greek commander Agamemnon has stolen a slave girl from him, but sends his friend Patroclus to fight in his, Achilles', armour. Hector, Priam's favourite son and bravest of the Trojans, kills Patroclus. Achilles avenges his friend's death by killing Hector and mutilating his body. Priam, now an old man, goes to Achilles as a suppliant and asks for Hector's body; Achilles consents. Troy eventually falls; Paris kills Achilles; Achilles' son Neoptolemus kills Priam. Hecuba, Helen and Hector's widow Andromache are left to be captured and enslaved by the victorious Greeks.

It is a grim story, though something more than an arbitrary series of vengeful killings. Tippett emphasizes two elements in it: choice and compassion. In Act One of *King Priam* we are shown three moments of decisive choice. First, Priam and Hecuba decide to have Paris put to death. (Hecuba has no doubts, but for Priam the choice is almost impossible. He reflects that he was once a child, unable to make a

Opposite, the composer in his music room, 1972.

c

choice, and he might have been killed by his parents, in which case Paris would not have been born. 'He is born because I lived. Shall I die that he may live?') Next, Paris, as an adolescent, chooses to leave his shepherd's life and go to Troy to become a young hero. Lastly, Paris, in love with Helen, is confronted with three goddesses and asked to favour one of them with the gift of a golden apple: the famous Judgement of Paris. Athene offers prowess on the battlefield, Hera the security of marriage, Aphrodite love. Paris chooses Aphrodite, and Helen. This last choice illustrates clearly the point Tippett is trying to make, that the apparent dilemma of choice is illusory, since the chosen course is inevitable. Paris must choose Helen, whatever the consequences: this is his nature, his destiny. In fact Priam's original choice was against his nature, as he realizes when he discovers that Paris was not killed as he had commanded. It was the guard's compassion that saved the child, and despite the fact that this act of compassion would seem to have brought about all the subsequent tragedy, compassion is seen as the only possible mitigating influence on the cruel course of history. The great scene of compassion in the opera occurs in the last act, when Priam goes to Achilles to beg for the body of Hector. The brutal Achilles is moved by Priam's supplication. He delivers up the body, and both men calmly accept their imminent deaths.

Priam is the central figure of the opera and none of the other characters is developed to the same extent, though Achilles is shown in a variety of guises: as supreme hero delivering his terrifying war-cry at the end of Act Two; as veteran warrior longing for home; as brutal avenger of Patroclus' death; finally, and most sympathetically, as simple, suffering human being capable of pity. Hector and Paris are two types of hero, Hector in war, Paris in love (Hector may despise Paris for unmanliness, but winning the most beautiful woman in the world who is a king's wife and daughter of Zeus into the bargain is no mean feat!). Andromache and Hecuba are two types of tragic heroine, both of them passionate and inflexible and neither of them able to understand the mysterious, numinous figure of Helen. Priam, having grown through the opera from young king to frail old man, in its last act becomes a visionary: once he has accepted his death he is able to transcend all human concerns. He has moved over from the human world of suffering to the divine, transfigured world; and it is fitting that the last person he speaks to, the only person he can now communicate with, is Helen, herself a demigoddess and an image of the soul as well as of sexual love. He dies with the words (taken from Yeats) 'I see mirrors myriad upon myriad moving the dark forms of creation'. Earlier, Hermes, the mediator between the human and divine worlds, has addressed the audience:

Do not imagine all the secrets of life can be known from a story.
O but feel the pity and the terror as Priam dies.

And feel it, he implies, as a purging of the emotions. Hermes goes on to sing of the healing power of music in an aria of great purity. So we are left at the end, not with unreconciled images of violence, but with images of healing and self-transcendence.

Three things make the musical language of *King Priam* sound quite new for Tippett. The first is the spareness of the texture. Tippett in this work denied himself the use of the luxuriant counterpoint that had marked all his previous music and especially *The Midsummer Marriage* and the works that immediately followed it. Instead, much of the texture consists of quite straightforward, though fairly dissonant, chordal writing: for the first time harmony is pre-eminent over counterpoint. Where he does use counterpoint it is rarely in more than three parts and frequently only two; while there are many places where the voice will be accompanied by only a single melodic line, as for example the toccata-like violin figuration which usually accompanies Hecuba, the solo cello for Andromache, and the guitar for most of Achilles' music. Ex. 17 overleaf shows the beginning of Hecuba's aria from the first scene of Act One: both vocal and instrumental lines match her assertive personality.

The piano is often used as a solo instrument and in Act Two it takes the place of the strings, which are silent throughout (the first scene of Act Three, by effective contrast, is scored entirely for strings alone). The full orchestra is hardly ever used, and those rare places where there is anything like a tutti sound, as for instance Priam's and Hecuba's regal exit in Act One, are thereby the more impressive. Similarly those few passages where the texture reverts to anything like Tippett's accustomed density, like the string writing at Paris's Act One entry or Helen's aria 'Let her rave' in Act Three, are also the

Ex. 17

more effective for their rarity. Though the actual melodic lines are for the most part characteristic Tippett, the bareness of their presentation makes them sound new and strange.

Secondly, the music is mostly non-developing, in marked contradiction to Tippett's earlier manner. Particular kinds of musics and tone-colours are associated with particular characters—we have already noted some of them—and these recur in the score largely unchanged. The result is that the texture of the score, in contrast to the symphonic character of *The Midsummer Marriage*, is much more like a huge mosaic.

Thirdly, because the music does not develop, it is no longer tonal in the traditional sense that Tippett's earlier music had been. There is still some use of key signatures and the individual sections generally have a tonal centre, even if the increased chromaticism of the harmony sometimes makes the sense of tonality rather tenuous. However, there is no clear tonal progression from one section to another and the overall effect is of a non-tonal work. This was a decisive break with the past, and Tippett was never again to return to traditional tonality in a large-scale work.

The special sound-world of *King Priam*—the ringing brass fanfares and the overall hardness (marvellously relaxed in the opening scene of Act Three)—gives it an extraordinarily haunting quality, and the compassionate and ultimately visionary quality of Act Three makes the opera a powerfully moving experience. For Tippett the writing of *King Priam* was a self-denying task: in this work and in the Second Piano Sonata, which is an epigrammatic companion-piece to the opera, he makes his most uncompromising stand against his earlier development and, in fact, against the kind of music that comes most naturally to him. It was a deliberate renewal of a sort which in our time is pre-eminently associated with Stravinsky; and Tippett's recognition of Stravinsky as the supreme modern master, as Beethoven is for him the supreme old master, undoubtedly helped confirm the rightness of his action. Later he was to re-absorb most of the elements of his style which he had temporarily abandoned, but now transformed and renewed, cleansed and refreshed.

CHAPTER NINE
The Public Composer

Tippett's finest music is the expression of the private composer delving into his inner self and translating into sound his deepest discoveries. But Tippett has a public side too; he believes strongly, as Britten did, that music should be useful, and that the composer should play a practical role in society. So all his composing life he has provided occasional music whenever he has been asked for it, much of it for voices, some of it for young people; while, as we have seen, he has been active for most of his life as a conductor both of his own and of others' music, and as a lecturer and broadcaster. In the 1960s he began to appear on television, and so to reach a still wider audience: the culmination of his television work has been the autobiographical 'One Pair of Eyes' film he made for the BBC in 1972, *Poets in a Barren Age*, in which he gave a succinct and eloquent analysis of the situation of the contemporary composer.

Tippett's work with amateurs during the 1930s has been touched upon, and some of the music he wrote for amateurs at that period has been mentioned: *The Village Opera*, for his Oxted choir; *Robin Hood*, for the Cleveland ironstone miners; the two children's operas he wrote with Christopher Fry: *Robert of Sicily* and *Seven at One Stroke*. All these pieces draw on the folk-idiom that was very much part of his language at that time. Since the 1940s numerous small pieces for particular occasions have been commissioned from Tippett by choirs, music societies, the BBC, and other bodies. To mention them all would be tedious, but they contain some minor masterpieces, like the motet *Plebs Angelica*, written for the choir of Canterbury Cathedral in 1943; *Dance, Clarion Air*, the outstanding contribution to the otherwise rather spineless collection of madrigals for the 1953 Coronation by ten contemporary composers, *A Garland for the Queen*; and the extraordinary *Magnificat and Nunc Dimittis* composed for St John's College, Cambridge, in 1961. To look at just one of these occasional works: in 1962 Tippett was asked to provide incidental music for a production of *The Tempest* at the Old Vic theatre, London. The three songs that Ariel sings and which have been set by many composers from Shakespeare's time up to the present were in Tippett's version originally scored for a small chamber ensemble, but he subsequently arranged the accompaniment for piano or harpsichord. Ex. 18 gives the second of them, 'Full Fathom Five'. Despite its simplicity, it is quintessential Tippett (and indeed Tippett has said that if only one of his pieces were to survive, he would be content if it were this song); the harmony at 'rich and strange', for example, is just that: a superb demonstration of how to make conventional chords sound fresh.

The two most substantial works for young people that Tippett has composed since the war have been the cantata *Crown of the Year* and *The Shires Suite* for chorus and orchestra. *Crown of the Year* was written in 1958 for the centenary of Badminton School for girls, Bristol, at the suggestion of Eric Walter White, whose daughter was a pupil there. The words were provided by Christopher Fry and appropriately related four British queens—Elizabeth I, Anne, Victoria and Elizabeth II—to the four seasons, beginning with spring. Each queen has a vocal movement which is preceded by a seasonal instrumental prelude; and each of the preludes contains a well-known tune, as a Bach chorale-prelude does. The writing is not easy, either for the voices (female voices only, of course) or for the instruments—recorders, oboe, clarinet, trumpet, percussion, piano and string quartet. So the piece has been virtually forgotten since its first performance—undeservedly, for it contains some fine things. One might single out 'Victoria Rules an Autumn Land', with its mellow scoring for alto voices, clarinet, cello and piano, and richly elaborate vocal lines; or the final chorus—whose calmly confident ending, suggesting new hope after our present-day winter, like the end of *A Child of Our Time*, recalls the Pastorale from the Corelli Fantasia composed a few years before.

In 1965 Tippett began an association with the Leicestershire Schools Symphony Orchestra and conducted this outstanding and

*These bars should be spoken; if preferred they may be sung however, in which case the given notes (F, E flat) apply.

Ex. 18

enthusiastic body of young musicians at a number of their concerts. *The Shires Suite* was composed between 1965 and 1970 for the orchestra and county school choirs; in its complete version it has five movements, of which the second and fourth are for orchestra alone. The Suite is based on canons: it opens with a lively version of the famous thirteenth-century canon 'Sumer is icumen in'. The central Cantata is a setting for chorus and orchestra of two extrovert canons by Byrd and Purcell and an introvert one by Alexander Goehr (this last was a sixtieth birthday present); and the final movement is a quiet and exceptionally beautiful version of Byrd's canon 'Non nobis, Domine'. This marriage of music from the past and Tippett's own latest style (by no means watered down for youthful consumption) makes a piquant blend.

CHAPTER TEN

Works of the 1960s

It was only in the 1960s that Tippett began to receive the kind of public recognition he deserved. It was reflected in the sudden flood of honours he received—not that they are of great importance to a composer concerned with the real issues of life, but they must have been some compensation for the years of semi-neglect. In 1959 he was awarded the CBE and in 1966 a knighthood. In 1964 he was made an honorary Doctor of Music at the University of Cambridge, the first of fourteen honorary doctorates he was to receive over the next dozen or so years. Records of his music began to appear in increasing numbers. Above all he found an ideal conductor in Colin Davis, who began to work miracles with the orchestral pieces, revealing their hidden glories, and triumphantly exorcizing the old accusations of amateurish technique that still lingered on.

In 1960 Tippett moved from Sussex to an old house with a formal garden on the edge of Corsham Park, near Bath in Wiltshire. He became associated with the Bath Festival and was its artistic director from 1969 until 1974.

The two major pieces that followed *King Priam* and grew out of its sound-world, the Second Piano Sonata and the Concerto for Orchestra, are perhaps Tippett's most experimental music, in so far as they are his most radical departures from the sonata/symphony archetype.* The Sonata is composed in a more extreme, and highly compressed, version of the opera's mosaic-like formal technique: it lasts only ten minutes, but is made up of thirty-eight sections of eight different musics, each music with its own tempo. The sections vary in length from one bar

---

* I should also mention here the short *Praeludium* for brass, bells and percussion, whose brilliant fanfare-like textures are closely related to the opening of *King Priam*.

to sixty-six: there is no real development within them; the development is in the way they are juxtaposed. The music is mostly as stark
as the most uncompromising parts of *King Priam*; though one section
has a flowing, lyrical theme whose fourths and A-flat tonality suddenly
recall the now distant world of the Piano Concerto:

Ex. 19

The Concerto for Orchestra is a more lyrical and relaxed work,
but its first movement is even more experimental in form, and the
King Priam device of dividing the orchestra into small groups is
carried a stage further. In re-forming the orchestra Tippett was doing
what many of his younger contemporaries were also doing, but he
surpasses almost all of them in the elegance of his scheme, which is
worth outlining in some detail. Tippett divides his orchestra (wind,
brass and percussion only in this movement) into small groups, three
sets of three; each group has its own music. The music of set 1 (flute
and harp; tuba and piano; three horns) is characterized by 'line and
flow' (Tippett's description); that of set 2 (timpani and piano; oboe,
cor anglais, bassoon and double bassoon; two trombones and percussion) by 'rhythm and dynamic punch'; that of set 3 (xylophone and
piano; clarinet and bass clarinet; two trumpets and side drum) by
'virtuosity and speed'. In the exposition the three sorts of music that
make up set 1 are heard in turn, then simultaneously; similarly sets

2 and 3. The rest of the movement is a big development or rather a series of what Tippett calls 'jam sessions', since (as we by now might expect) each group's music remains essentially unchanged; but all kinds of collisions take place between the various groups. The result is rather like a kaleidoscope: the patterns go on revolving and shifting, though the material remains the same. Towards the end the opening flute and harp bars keep reasserting themselves, and they close the movement. The whole process has seemed logical and satisfying.

The slow movement is in absolute contrast, being scored for the hitherto silent strings (with piano and harp), and consisting of an almost unbroken, highly elaborate—even for Tippett—melodic line, moving gradually upwards from cellos to violas and finally to violins (who do not enter until this point, half-way through the movement), followed by a densely contrapuntal discussion of the melody. The first part of the movement is the longest and richest so far of Tippett's string ascents, surpassing those in the Corelli Fantasia and the Second Symphony and anticipating passages in *The Vision of Saint Augustine* in the intensity of its sustained ecstatic mood. This movement is one of Tippett's supreme achievements.

The finale is a rondo with a bounding trumpet theme. It will make an interesting comparison to put alongside Tippett's tune (Ex. 20a) the main theme of the finale of Britten's Cello Symphony (Ex. 20b) composed at about the same time—also for trumpet, also accompanied by a single string line (Tippett has all the violins, Britten just the solo cello). Though the styles of the two composers remain, as always, sharply differentiated, Tippett has now joined Britten in a liking for clear, uncluttered textures. The orchestration of the Concerto for Orchestra's finale is very like parts of *King Priam*, from which it also borrows several of its themes. The end (like the ends of both previous movements) is indecisive, it just stops; but this is not a piece much concerned with progressions, even in the slow movement, which is rather the gradual unfolding of a single idea. It is, with the Second Piano Sonata, Tippett's most abstract piece; his least worldly. It is not at all concerned with extra-musical ideas, rather it celebrates the act of making music itself—and could anything be more appropriate in a work dedicated to Benjamin Britten?

Tippett's next important work, his second oratorio *The Vision of*

(a) Tippett

Ex. 20

Saint Augustine, which he composed between 1963 and 1965, is in one sense the most ambitious thing he has ever attempted. It aims at describing the indescribable: Saint Augustine's vision of eternity, as it is recorded in his *Confessions*. It is the culmination of that strain in Tippett's music which reaches out towards a state of ecstasy, of timelessness. Like a number of English artists—Vaughan Williams, Holst, Wordsworth, Samuel Palmer—Tippett has strong temperamental leanings towards nature mysticism; though he stands closest of all to Blake in his visionary outlook and in his sense of wonder. Saint Augustine's vision, however, is of the rarer kind experienced by ascetic mystics; in his case it came about after a long and painful struggle to overcome his natural sensuality, which he believed to be wholly evil, and to accept the Christian faith. He recounts how, five days before his mother's death, discussing with her 'the eternal life of the saints . . . we came to our own souls and went beyond them . . . while we were thus talking of eternal life and panting for it we touched it for a moment with a supreme effort of our heart'. The vision as such is not one that Tippett himself would claim to understand from personal experience: the chorus are his mouthpiece at the very end of the work when they whisper 'I count not myself to have apprehended'.

Music can evoke the idea of timelessness more powerfully than words, in spite of the fact that every piece of music is strictly defined by its duration in time. Eliot's words from *Four Quartets* come to mind: 'Only through time time is conquered.' Music too can hint at meanings beyond the expressive capacity of words. And so Tippett's oratorio may give us a clearer insight into Saint Augustine's vision than Augustine's own attempt at description. Appropriately, the two supreme moments in *The Vision of Saint Augustine* occur when the voices break off and instruments take over, at the end of each of the first two parts. The oratorio's first two parts are both huge expansions of the formal idea of the ascent, with the solo baritone narrating (in Latin) Saint Augustine's words and the chorus commenting, taking up his words and interpolating their own from the Bible and from Saint Ambrose's hymn 'Deus, Creator Omnium'. In Part One the climax is a joyous, cosmic dance for the orchestra in $\frac{6}{8}$ rhythm. Part Two begins again quietly and grows slowly towards the moment of vision, which is signalled by a great outburst of alleluias for chorus and orchestra; then the solo baritone leads us into the orchestral coda: slowly pulsing, melismatic music, recalling the middle movement of the Concerto for Orchestra. The third part attempts a summing up: within time we can only experience the timeless momentarily; if the vision could be prolonged this would be the eternal life of the Saints— in other words, Heaven. The grand choral climax of Part Two is repeated and the chorus add to it an exultant 'Lift up your heads O ye gates, and be ye lifted up ye everlasting doors'. It is difficult to judge *The Vision of Saint Augustine* by conventional standards, as it aims beyond the reach of the earthly possible; but it is a tribute to the power of Tippett's music that we are constantly made to feel on the edge of revelation, and just occasionally we forget ourselves and, to quote from Eliot's *Four Quartets* again, we 'are the music while the music lasts'.

CHAPTER ELEVEN

The Knot Garden

Tippett's third opera *The Knot Garden* is a different kind of work again from the first two. To draw a not implausible analogy with Mozart, if *The Midsummer Marriage* were his *Magic Flute* and *King Priam* his *Idomeneo*, then *The Knot Garden* would be his *Così fan tutte*. This is an opera about personal relationships in the modern world, and how relationships that have gone wrong may eventually come right. Its motto is a line from Shakespeare's *All's Well That Ends Well* (which might be a subtitle for *The Knot Garden*): 'simply the thing I am shall make me live.' Shakespeare is the most important influence on Tippett's libretto for *The Knot Garden*, and Tippett has said that he regards Shakespeare as a kind of cauldron of material and ideas, which he feels entitled to draw on in the same way as the Greek dramatists drew on Homer's *Iliad*. Other figures too were influential. This passage from a talk which Tippett gave before the first performance of *The Knot Garden* at Covent Garden (in December 1970) will explain the somewhat complicated literary traditions behind the opera:

The traditions are twofold, and it is the first that is the most difficult to substantiate—that is to say, most difficult without leading everyone too far afield. I shall pick my theatrical examples therefore as carefully as I can. The prime example, it seems to me, is Shaw's *Heartbreak House*. This is a play about a small set of characters, gathered together somewhat arbitrarily in a house and garden, where they play out a pattern or game of cross-relationships. There is very little story-line or pure dramatic situation, and the action of the play is only ended when all the possible cross-relationships are exhausted and all games with one another played.

This is the essence of this type of theatrical piece. The story-line, if there is one, does not decide the shape of the action, but the relationships and the games. Some of the characters are changed by these games, others, we feel, will go on re-playing them for ever.

There are innumerable examples of this genre in the modern theatre. I will name only one: *Who's afraid of Virginia Woolf?* of Edward Albee. Because here the cross-relationships are reduced to those of only four people (so that the art is fantastically economical and pure) and because the older couple know they are playing out the ritual games and say so. What these games might be brings me to the second tradition.

We have seen in recent years a continuing interest in the late ironic comedies of Shakespeare, such as *Measure for Measure* or *All's Well That Ends Well*. These plays have been called Comedies of Forgiveness (there is a long late medieval Christian tradition of such plays before Shakespeare) and their main definition is that while through most of the play's length the relationships are very wrong indeed, there is a final, often quite arbitrary, scene of forgiveness; in this forgiveness lies any hope we have of the relationships, or the social situation, going over from wrong to right. For my own purposes I include Shakespeare's *The Tempest* in the list of such Comedies of Forgiveness. And it is from *The Tempest* that I have taken the 'games' for the last act of *The Knot Garden*. Five of the seven characters in the opera play short charades as though they were characters in *The Tempest*, playing scenes which might have happened or which Shakespeare just lets Prospero or Miranda speak about but we do not see. In *The Knot Garden* there are four of such 'games' to play and when they are over only forgiveness offers us some hope.

> If for a timid moment
> We submit to love
> Exit from the inner cage
> Turn each to each to all

as the final ensemble has it.

I don't think we can expect much beyond 'a timid moment' considering the kind of folk we now know ourselves to be and how little we now believe in Miranda's 'brave new world'.

And that is what *The Knot Garden* is about.

With this background in mind, we can turn to the actual events of the opera. Tippett's seven characters are: a married couple, Faber and Thea, in whose garden the action takes place; their adolescent ward,

Flora; Thea's sister, Denise, a 'dedicated freedom-fighter' who has just been released from prison; a homosexual, or, as is later revealed, bisexual couple, Mel, a black writer, and Dov, a white musician; and Mangus, an analyst. Mangus announces at the start that he is to 'play Prospero', who 'put them all to rights'. He seems to be modelled in part on Harcourt-Reilly in Eliot's *The Cocktail Party* (though his name derives from Boss Mangan in *Heartbreak House*), and indeed the influence of Eliot's verse-plays, though Tippett does not especially acknowledge it in connection with *The Knot Garden*, remains strong. Mangus will be the still centre around whom the other characters revolve. All of the others have assumed artificial roles for self-protection. Faber's and Thea's marriage has broken down and Thea has retreated into the private world of her garden; while Faber, whose masculine pride has been wounded by Thea's rejecting him, plays at flirtation, at first with the vulnerable Flora, later even with Dov. Flora would rather retreat into her childhood than face growing up. Mel's and Dov's relationship is also at breaking point, and their insecurity is evident from their appearance in fancy dress disguise as Caliban and Ariel, and their inability at first to speak except in caricature. Even Denise—whose entrance midway through Act One, 'half-majestic, half-sinister . . . twisted or otherwise disfigured from the effects of torture', has the catalytic power to begin the process of transformation —is playing a role of sorts, that of martyr; though her terrible serious-ness and the immensity of her ordeal give her a kind of exaggerated reality against which the others' problems seem doubly artificial.

Denise's electrifying appearance sets in motion—galvanizes, as it were—the fantastic series of confrontations in the second act, where the garden is transformed into a labyrinth, the 'knot garden' of the title (knot gardens were formal mazes in Elizabethan gardens). The characters are whirled on and off, and personal tensions reach their peak, explode and reform. The calming-down at the end of this act, where Flora and Dov, left alone together, begin to find their own identities in song—Flora in Schubert's 'Die liebe Farbe' from *Die schöne Müllerin*, Dov with a song of his own—is a complement to the blues ensemble at the end of Act One which was the immediate response—the only possible one in the circumstances—to Denise's long and painful aria. And just as Mel had indicated by his final, half-dismissive 'Sure, baby' that the blues was only a temporary solution, so he enters at the end of Act Two to counter Dov's song with 'I taught you that'; and the rose garden which had begun to grow out of the chaos of the labyrinth while Dov was singing and Flora, 'the bud that hasn't opened', beginning to blossom out, now quickly fades.

A possible solution appears only in Act Three after the charades presided over by Mangus-Prospero. Here Mel and Dov resume their Caliban/Ariel roles, Faber plays Ferdinand, and Flora, Miranda. The games over, the characters can at last become their natural selves. As Tippett indicates, he is only able to present a qualified optimism: the romantic certainty of *The Midsummer Marriage* is no longer possible for him. As Judith Hubback wrote in a recent article (in *The Listener*) on Jungian psychology: 'It is more congenial to our late twentieth-century minds to consider processes and stages, and to have aims, but not to assume they will be conclusively reached.' The characters depart, undoubtedly to face many more problems in the future, but, we feel, at least better able to cope with them. Mel leaves with Denise: we hope she has accepted him as a man as well as a cause. Dov and Flora go separately but having drawn some strength from their encounter and both now able to act freely. Finally, Thea and Faber are reconciled in a short closing scene where they appear, like Mark and Jenifer, as an archetypal couple; the visionary in Tippett once again illuminates an elemental human situation with music of great radiance.

The most striking characteristic of *The Knot Garden* is its concentration. The three acts last in all only about an hour and a half; there are, however, no less than thirty-two scenes, some of which are naturally extremely short and some of which follow one another very abruptly. The technique is similar to that of film, and Tippett uses the term 'dissolve' to denote the break-up of the stage picture at one point in time and its immediate re-formation at another. There is also, as in film, an increased reliance on the visual event, which makes *The Knot Garden* more difficult than usual to appreciate away from a stage production.

Despite its conciseness, there is still a place for extended set-pieces. Denise's Act One aria is the largest and most striking; there is also Dov's strophic song at the end of Act Two and, on a smaller scale, Thea's aria of self-discovery, 'I am no more afraid', in Act Three, and Mel and Denise's duet in Act Two. These places are the still points in a deliriously turning world, necessary moments of stability in a score that otherwise moves with bewildering rapidity. The two big ensembles for all the characters, the blues finale to Act One and 'If for a timid moment' in Act Three, are nicely contrasted. The blues, coming at the point of maximum confusion, has the densest textured writing in the score, and wildly independent vocal lines, each character singing out his or her private anguish; while the Act Three ensemble, coming at the moment of reconciliation, symbolizes it happily by having all the characters, for the first and only time, sing together in block harmonies.

The language of the libretto ranges widely from Tippett's familiar 'high-style' blank verse derived from Yeats and Eliot through everyday prose dialogue to contemporary jargon and slang. Thus he has incorporated catch-phrases such as 'The beautiful and damned' and 'Stop the world, I want to get off', which are in fact now rather out-of-date but, as he has confidently pointed out, won't sound so in a hundred years' time. There is also a good deal of actual quotation from *The Tempest*. The result is that the libretto reads rather like *The Waste Land*, and the mixture of styles makes it considerably more disconcerting at first glance than *The Midsummer Marriage* or *King Priam*. The concision too means that each phrase is thrown more strongly into relief; there is virtually no padding.

As for the musical language, Tippett has moved on a stage further from *The Vision of Saint Augustine* to a rich synthesis of all his previous styles, together with some (for him) innovations. For instance, the opera begins with a twelve-note row, which recurs several times, though there are only exploratory attempts at using it structurally: like Britten and Shostakovich in some of their later works, Tippett has seized on the note-row as a useful device, but no more than that. The formal novelties of *King Priam* and its associated works have been absorbed and integrated. The dramatic technique of throwing the characters together in various combinations in the Labyrinth of Act Two makes an interesting parallel with the musical technique of the first movement of the Concerto for Orchestra. If the textures are never, by virtue of the overall concision, allowed to flower as pro-lifically as in *The Midsummer Marriage*, nevertheless they are luxuriant enough to make *King Priam* seem an outgrown stage of austere self-denial. The comprehensiveness of *The Knot Garden*'s musical language may be illustrated by an example from near the start of the opera. The dreamy horns that accompany Thea's first appearance remind us of the world of *The Midsummer Marriage*, while the harmony shows the influence of *King Priam*; but the pronounced angularity of the vocal line is new.

Ex. 21

Ex. 22

Another fresh device in this score, and one which was to become still more important in subsequent works, is that of allusion: to the music of other composers—the Schubert song that Flora sings; to contemporary folk-music—the protest song 'We Shall Overcome' which steals into the Mel/Denise Act Two duet (see Ex. 22); as well as to Tippett's own earlier work, the Shakespeare songs 'Full Fathom Five', and 'Come unto these Yellow Sands', which are used in Act Three. The emergence of 'We Shall Overcome' from a polytonal string texture (in Ex. 22) recalls similar passages in Charles Ives, a composer who began to interest Tippett greatly during the 1960s. This and other aspects of the score point to the increasing influence of America on Tippett's music, which I shall deal with in the next chapter.

The Knot Garden is not an easy work to come to terms with. It profoundly disturbs our preconceptions as to how characters in opera should behave and what they should sing. It refuses so far to settle down and become a modern classic: time will be needed yet before this can happen. For a composer in his mid-sixties, it was an extraordinarily daring departure to treat an old preoccupation of his—the reconciliation of opposites and the possibility of individuation—in such a new and provocative way. Once again Tippett's capacity for self-renewal had shown itself, and suggested new directions for the next decade.

CHAPTER TWELVE

A Language for Our Time

The background to Tippett's recent music—the range of references and allusions—is more complex than ever, making it difficult to treat each piece adequately in a short space. *The Knot Garden* inaugurated a series of works whose main characteristic is their comprehensiveness: Tippett is drawing all the threads of his past together as well as continuing to explore the present, and the resultant mixture is of a sometimes bewildering richness. But there are two preoccupations that stand out —one familiar, the other new: with Beethoven, and with America.

Since 1965, when Tippett made his first visit to the United States as composer in residence at the Aspen Festival in Colorado, America has become important to him both as a place and as a symbol. He has made many subsequent visits to the States, to conduct, hear his music, lecture and sightsee. His music has suddenly become very popular there. The American experience has been for him in the first place an expansion of vision: a conscious reaching out, by someone who is so much an Englishman and a European, to embrace a culture different in many ways from his own, perhaps in the realization that Europe is culturally no longer self-sufficient; that the old world now needs the new as much as the new world has always needed the old.

At the same time he has made his own response to the enormous phenomenon of American popular music, which has affected composers as far removed from its milieu as Stravinsky and Berg, as well as providing a basic language for figures like Gershwin and Weill. In its various forms—jazz, popular song, rock—American popular music is something few composers this century have been able totally to ignore, and indeed it has now become the musical vernacular for Europe as well as the United States. Tippett had been familiar with jazz since the late 1920s and came especially to love the blues; and as the relevance of folk-song to his music has receded, so the blues have come to replace folk-song as a vernacular basis for his musical language.

Already in the late 1930s the 'feel' of jazz was infiltrating his music: the Concerto for Double String Orchestra, for instance, which Aaron Copland told him he had thought was a piece of American music when he first heard it. We have noted the crucial impact of the spiritual 'Steal Away' on *A Child of Our Time*, and Tippett's decision to include spirituals in his oratorio. But the true 'Americanization' of Tippett's music does not begin until *The Knot Garden*. There is the electric guitar music associated with Mel and Dov, who might be themselves (though it is not stated) Americans; and especially the big blues number that ends Act One, and Dov's song 'I was born in a big town' in Act Two. The latter was the starting point for the *Songs for Dov*, which Tippett wrote immediately after the opera; a parallel piece, but a weightier one, to the *Songs for Achilles* which came out of *King Priam*.

Songs for Dov was conceived of as the music that Dov, the young itinerant musician, might have composed and sung. It is the testament of someone who has travelled widely and through a range of experience to arrive at some kind of maturity; a familiar story of the romantic outsider, familiar from a number of nineteenth-century song cycles. Today, however, he is most likely to be found in the world of rock music—in the person of someone like Bob Dylan. And in fact Dov's language, richly allusive, with references to Shakespeare, Goethe, Homer and Pasternak side by side with 'pop' colloquialisms, could be compared not too fancifully with Dylan's blend of exotic imagery derived from Rimbaud and Ginsberg together with more straightforward blues and folk. Dylan's own musical language is, of course, very simple (though devastatingly effective); whereas Dov-Tippett can allude not only to blues and boogie-woogie (again with the help of the electric guitar) but to Beethoven, Wagner, Mussorgsky and Tippett himself. But the parallel can be extended, for Dylan and Dov reach essentially the same solution after disillusion in the city and 'on the road'. Dylan eventually found solace in country music after the nadir of bleak urban songs like 'Desolation Row'; Dov sings, quoting from Boris Pasternak:

Surely it is my calling
To see that the distances do not lose heart
And that beyond the limits of the town
The Earth shall not feel lonely.

In other words (Tippett's): 'one of the tasks of, shall we say, lyric poets of our period, might be just to sustain the pastoral metaphor, in its deep sense, against the ephemeralities of town fashions.'

Dov, in singing out his troubles towards a solution of some kind, anticipates one of the chief themes of the Third Symphony, possibly the most important of all Tippett's recent pieces. It brings us back also to his continuing preoccupation with Beethoven.

The title of Tippett's 'One Pair of Eyes' television film was derived from a line by the great German poet Hölderlin, a contemporary of Beethoven: 'What use are poets in a barren age?' This is a challenge to which Tippett has felt compelled to give an answer: 'What does this music—or any music—do within our present society, and what do I think I am doing by composing it?' If Hölderlin could pose his question at a time when Beethoven was writing his Ninth Symphony, how much more urgent it would seem to be today. Few artists of Hölderlin's generation would have agreed that their age was barren; for most it was a time of faith and optimism, when Shelley could proclaim that 'poets are the unacknowledged legislators of the world' (unacknowledged, maybe, but none the less influential for that), and Beethoven could feel he was speaking to all men, and set with audacity Schiller's invocation to the goddess Joy:

Alle Menschen werden Brüder
Wo dein sanfter Flügel weilt.

How much meaning does the finale of Beethoven's Ninth Symphony have today for us, who have seen how the confident claims of the early Romantics have turned out? What they prophesied now seems hardly more than fantasy; yet, in spite of everything, we are reluctant to admit that all their hopes were false. And if our age is barren, the responsibility the artist bears for showing us how we may still be joyful, how we can still praise, is greater than ever. With this in mind, we can approach the Third Symphony, which Tippett wrote in 1970–2 at a time, it may be mentioned, when disillusion in the Western world was at a peak.

As with so many of Tippett's works, the exact moment of the Symphony's conception can be pinpointed. During a concert of contemporary music in Edinburgh in 1965, Tippett began to reflect on how so much of today's music has no sense of movement—harmonic, rhythmic or melodic; and how he himself could never write such absolutely static music unless it were contrasted with its opposite. This was not, of course, a new insight: it was his old concern with making a whole out of contrasting and conflicting parts; and also with dynamism as an essential element: the 'Beethoven allegro' obsession, to which he has returned again and again with a fresh solution.

The Symphony opens with an allegro immediately presenting two types of dynamic music: sharp, barking brass chords marked 'Arrest' contrasting with leaping, exuberant music for strings and wind marked 'Movement'. Tippett has used the metaphor of the pull and thrust of a jet engine to describe these two kinds of music. They alternate separately five times in all—the sections becoming longer with each repetition—until in the final 'movement' section the 'arrest' music abruptly intrudes and the combination provokes a violent climax, which cuts off at its peak to reveal the slow movement. In this symphony of contrasts, the slow movement is at the furthest possible remove from the allegro, being almost completely static, with seemingly endless revolutions of quiet phrases for solo strings and wind, and bell-like percussion sounds. Tippett has compared this music to a windless night sky, and indeed the music seems suspended in air. Then, in total contrast, we suddenly descend to the depths of the string section (into the sea, in Tippett's imagery) and one of his richest, most-densely textured ascents begins, the aspiring contrapuntal lines flowering into semiquavers. The rest of the movement alternates fragments of his ascent with the night sky music, paralleling the contrasts of the allegro, and recalling the similar process in the slow ment of the Second Symphony.

Part Two opens with a mosaic-like scherzo, with five different types of music juggled together in a more abrasive way than in the similarly planned first movement of the Concerto for Orchestra. The effect is, as Tippett admits, rather like an Ives piece. At the point of maximum density comes the greatest contrast and the greatest shock: a direct quotation of the opening of the finale of Beethoven's Ninth Symphony. Now we know where we stand: this is to be an open confrontation with the *Ode to Joy*. Tippett must challenge it; for Beethoven and Schiller were wrong: men are not brothers. So in place of Beethoven's confident chorus a solo soprano sings a set of blues, beginning with Tippett's tribute to the blues he values above all others: Bessie Smith's 'St Louis Blues', with the young Louis Armstrong playing the cornet. Ex. 23 overleaf shows the start of Tippett's blues, with Armstrong's part metamorphosed into a flugelhorn solo which comments on each line of the verse, just as in the original. The Blake-like words are Tippett's own.

The first three blues are fairly straightforward: songs of acceptance, of physical and sexual pleasure, of compassion. The fourth song, much more complex, and a dramatic *scena* rather than a blues, tries to come to terms with the *Ode to Joy* by interpreting its message in the context of today. It is prefaced by a restatement of the opening of Beethoven's finale, and interspersed with further quotations from it. The soprano begins:

> They sang that when she waved her wings,
> The Goddess Joy would make us one.
> And did my brother die of frost-bite in the camp?
> And was my sister charred to cinders in the oven?

This is the final contrast and the one most fraught with difficulty. Can we accept man's capacity for evil (so evident in our time) alongside his capacity for good? The pain in the world alongside the joy? But what else can we do if we are to go on living? Tippett ends his poem with Martin Luther King's 'I have a dream': the dream that man can still heal the suffering world by love.

> What though the dream crack!
> We shall remake it . . .
> We sense a huge compassionate power
> To heal
> To love.

If no Ode to Joy is possible, Tippett offers an Ode to Compassion. The music is turbulent, then still and suspenseful: underneath, one

Ex. 23

Ex.24

senses great strength. There is no definite conclusion: aggression (brass chords like those at the beginning of the piece) alternates with tenderness (blues-inflected string chords); the strings have the last word—though only just. There is still hope, even if it is fragile.

The Third Symphony took over two years to write, and Tippett thought that his next piece, the Third Piano Sonata, written for the young pianist Paul Crossley, would be a relaxation after the strain of composing the Symphony: in the event, it was not quite so simple. With the Sonata we return to strictly classical values, but stay in the shadow of Beethoven. Tippett calls this his 'late Beethoven sonata'; and the slow movement certainly, with its incandescent textures and the showers of trills in its final variation, has affinities with several of Beethoven's late sonata movements, as well as with Tippett's own Piano Concerto. The outer, fast movements are almost entirely linear (we have moved to the opposite pole from the Second Piano Sonata) and the last movement is virtually all two-part writing, so that the occasional intrusions of loud repeated chords are a real surprise. Ex. 24 shows the opening of the first variation of the slow movement.

CHAPTER THIRTEEN

The Composer Now

Tippett today lives in a fine modern house on top of a hill a few miles away from his former home at Corsham. From his study window a wide expanse of unspoilt country stretches north-west towards Gloucestershire. The house is sparsely furnished: there are a few pictures, a few shelves of books; Tippett has always lived frugally and his recent relative prosperity has not expressed itself in material possessions. His only real luxury is a small swimming pool. Nearby is a lawn where he regularly beats his friends at croquet—he is something of an expert at this deceptively mild pastime.

His life is nicely divided between extended periods of composition and long visits abroad which are usually a combination of work (conducting and lecturing) and holiday (fairly energetic sightseeing). In addition to his many trips to America he has recently visited Australia and the Far East. When composing, he works a five-day week, with free week-ends. His working days are simple and regular: three hours of composition between breakfast and lunch; in the afternoon relaxation, reading, writing letters, going for walks, thinking out his music in advance; after supper usually television—he is particularly addicted to American crime series. The deterioration of his eyesight over the past few years—though now halted—has restricted him a little, but he copes with it well: one of the few obvious signs is the special large-scale manuscript paper on which he now writes his scores.

In July 1977 his fourth opera *The Ice Break* was given its première at Covent Garden in a spectacular production by Sam Wanamaker, the original producer of *King Priam*. In contrast to the intimate, private world of *The Knot Garden*, *The Ice Break* is a return to the public arena with a vengeance, much of the action taking place in the hectic surroundings of an airport lounge, and with the Chorus playing as important a role again as in *The Midsummer Marriage*. Though it is not specified, the location is clearly the United States: Tippett's American involvement has led him to write an opera fundamentally American in feeling and related to a characteristically American situation; though its themes are also universal ones. The overriding theme is racial conflict, and the Chorus are cast as a hostile, slogan-shouting crowd, black against white: they are incited by the champion black athlete Olympion (a vociferous advocate of black power) to a race riot in which several of the principal characters, including Olympion himself, are killed. At the same time as the airport crowd are awaiting the arrival of Olympion, a Russian wife, Nadia, is preparing for the return of her husband Lev, who has just been released after twenty years in the camps. Their son, Yuri, who has never known his father and can show no love towards him when they meet, is seriously injured in the riot; he is tended by a black nurse, Hannah, who was Olympion's girlfriend. (Yuri's own—white—girlfriend Gayle has been killed in the riot: her provocative flirtation with Olympion was one of its chief causes.)

In the third act, Nadia dies as she hears in a vision the sound of the ice breaking in the Russian spring of her childhood. Yuri is symbolic-ally reborn, cracked out of a plaster shell, and is reconciled to his father; but not before we have had a visit from a 'psychedelic mes-senger', Astron, who, while disclaiming the role of a saviour, delivers his gnomic panacea to the chorus, now peacefully united on a 'drug trip':

> Take care for the Earth
> God will take care for himself.

As can be seen from this brief introduction, Tippett has once again produced a work of contemporary significance out of a plethora of new and even bizarre sources—Solzhenitsyn, *West Side Story*, rock musicals, black power, TV soap opera, UFOs: the list could be extended. Despite its allusive richness, *The Ice Break* is, however, even more concise than *The Knot Garden*, with a total playing time of no more than an hour and a quarter. Though this brevity ensures dramatic tightness—particularly in Act One where short scenes between Nadia and Yuri, then Nadia and Lev are most effectively cross-cut with the chorus rushing in and out to greet Olympion's arrival—it is clearly disadvantageous to the portrayal of character in depth. While Nadia, Lev and Hannah develop into fully human figures with whom we can readily sympathize, there is hardly time for some of the other characters—Olympion, Gayle, Doctor Luke—to emerge as anything more than strip-cartoon figures (though the deaths of Olympion and Gayle are somehow made more inevitable and 'right' by presenting them as cyphers who can speak only in slogans and clichés). There are problems, too, with the attempt at a change of tone in Act Three. The predominant mood of the music of the first two acts is dark and tense; the characteristic orchestral sound is of brooding cellos and basses, punctuated by ominous bass-drum strokes. Tension mounts towards the climactic episodes of Act Two: Hannah's superb 'Blue night of my soul' aria, an inspired successor to the great series of introspective monologues for female voice in Tippett's operas, from Sosostris's aria in *The Midsummer Marriage* through Helen's 'Let her rave' in *King Priam* to Denise's aria in *The Knot Garden*; and the race riot which immediately follows it. The music of compassion at the end of the act is too insubstantial to effect much of a change, as is also the music for the 'psychedelic trip' in Act Three—which in any case is not one of Tippett's happiest dramatic inspirations. So the final scenes of hope seem even more tentative than the end of the Third Symphony; perhaps appropriately enough, since the huge questions that Tippett poses here certainly admit of no easy solutions.

Hard on the heels of *The Ice Break* came the first performance, in Chicago, of the Fourth Symphony by the Chicago Symphony Orchestra—who had commissioned it—under Sir Georg Solti. This is a return to an abstract, purely instrumental conception of the symphony; but its thirty-minute single movement marks a new formal direction, which future works are likely to develop. In planning it Tippett was influenced more by the Strauss symphonic poems and by Elgar's *Falstaff* than by other one-movement symphonies such as Sibelius's Seventh; and the Fourth Symphony has other affinities with the symphonic poem in its broadly existential programme: Tippett has said that it is a 'birth-to-death piece'. It begins and ends with sounds

71445

of breathing; to produce these the score indicates a wind-machine, though this is not quite the sound Tippett had in mind and in recent performances a synthesizer has been used to better effect. The orchestra is the largest he has yet used, with a big brass section of six horns, three tumpets, three trombones and two tubas and some sonorous ensemble writing for them. There is a rugged grandeur about the work that recalls such American symphonies as Roy Harris's Third or Copland's Third, while its broad lyricism is on an American scale too. It is a fine testament to the continuing vigour of Tippett's creative powers.

What of the future? A Fourth String Quartet is just finished, a Concerto for String Trio and Orchestra planned, and, on the horizon, and beginning to take shape in his mind, is the huge culminating choral work that will sum up the whole of his creative life. Enough here to keep him fully occupied until he reaches his eighties. Meanwhile, as he approaches seventy-five, he shows no sign of becoming the venerable Old Master that his age might suggest; rather he remains the eternally youthful dispenser of joyful wisdom, the man of wise experience who has yet had to sacrifice none of his curiosity or his innocence.

Epilogue

It might seem premature to try to sum up Tippett's achievement while he is still so much alive and active among us. Nevertheless, since his earliest published works are now over forty years old—and he himself feels very detached from them—we can put these at least into some kind of historical perspective, and can go on to bring his music as a whole into provisional focus.

Tippett's musical language in his early works is markedly conservative, even in the then context of English music. Of the major Continental innovators, Hindemith alone is a felt presence in Tippett's early music; and it is significant that by the 1930s Hindemith was in the process of renouncing what he had come to believe were the sins of a misspent avant-garde youth and adopting a traditionalist stance, which he attempted to justify by massive theorizing. To judge from the music alone, we could well imagine (though we should in fact be wrong) that Tippett was then unaware of Stravinsky (whose influence on other members of his generation such as Walton or Constant Lambert had already been considerable), and also of Bartók or Schoenberg. What is certainly apparent, and true, is that there is a strong continuity with the previous generation of English composers, Vaughan Williams in particular. This is emphasized by Tippett's belief in the continuing validity of folk-music as a musical vernacular, at a time when such a belief was very rapidly going out of fashion.

Tippett's conservative beginnings are, however, misleading; for he was to become a very different kind of composer from Edmund Rubbra or Gerald Finzi, to name but two thoroughgoing conservatives among his contemporaries. Yet certainly his overriding aim in the late 1930s was conservative *par excellence*: it was no less than the re-creation of classical tonality. Such an aim tells us much about Tippett's confidence in his own powers, a confidence which was largely to be justified by the achievement of the next decade. In an article that he wrote in 1938 (I have already quoted from it on p.52), Tippett traces the degeneration of the tonal system since Beethoven's time, remarking that: 'the tonal system related to sonata form is a highly polarized system. Modern people are not polarized, they are split. Since the nineteenth century composers have ceased to produce the sort of themes that demanded Beethoven's clarity of tonal structure.' Clearly Tippett saw his personal quest for psychological wholeness, which he was undertaking through Jungian self-analysis, as related to a necessary rediscovery of classical, i.e. Beethoven's, tonal values. The re-creation of a classical language was achieved with remarkable success in the works of the 1940s, culminating in *The Midsummer Marriage*, perhaps the most tonally stable of all large-scale works written this century. Its resplendent A major close (with a Wagnerian sustained final triad) is a precise musical parallel to the psychological stability that Mark and Jenifer have attained. In all the music of this period, the final cadence on to the tonic triad has the unforced strength of a true classical work. Tippett's classicism sounds absolutely natural: out-wardly directed emotions are expressed in music that is both gracefully lyrical and vigorously athletic. In contrast, the neoclassicism of Stravinsky, despite its brilliance, seems studied and inhibited; it never quite lets go. Tippett's music of the 1940s comes very close at times to the classically poised world of Beethoven; or, in a wider context, to that of Goethe, who, in a similar spirit, revitalized the classical elegaic couplet:

> Froh empfind ich mich nun auf klassischem Boden begeistert;
>   Vor- und Mitwelt spricht lauter und reizender mir.

> (How happy and inspired I feel now on classical soil;
>   Both the past and the present speak to me with more eloquence
>   and charm.)

By the mid 1950s, Tippett realized that he could do no more with traditional tonality without repeating himself; he also felt a need to expand his musical vocabulary. It was at this point that he turned (there is some irony here) to the neoclassical Stravinsky of the 1930s and 1940s, just at the period when Stravinsky himself was leaving neoclassicism behind and turning towards serialism in an attempt to reinvigorate his own language. In Tippett's Second Symphony of 1956–7, the first major piece to show Stravinskian influence, the writing is generally more sectional, the tonality more static, the harmony more astringent. But the music still has a more continuous, integrated flow—it is more symphonic—than one ever finds in Stravinsky. This is not to say that Tippett is a better composer than Stravinsky; only that Tippett has done things with Stravinskian language that Stravinsky himself was incapable of doing, just as, say, Bruckner used Wagnerian language in a quite different way from Wagner.

Tippett has continued to generate genuine symphonic movement in subsequent works up to and including his most recent, the Fourth Symphony; he has managed to do so despite his gradual abandonment of the tonal language which he had so impressively mastered. Whether his present synthetic language, with its Americanized, blues-based vernacular and wide allusive range, and its use of tonal gestures within a generally non-tonal background (one can usefully employ Rudolph Réti's term 'pantonality' to describe it), is a wholly adequate substitute for the classical tonality of his earlier works is an intriguing question; but one which it is too early yet to answer with any certainty.

The grammar of Tippett's language is an obvious key to his individuality, but his tone of voice is no less distinctive. The exalted, ecstatic tone of Tippett's most idiosyncratic music is what singles him out from almost all his contemporaries. The only figure with whom he can properly be compared is Messiaen, though they are very different, both as composers and as representatives of two totally distinct cultures. Messiaen's Roman Catholicism, awesomely transcendent and at the same time deeply sensuous, pervades and characterizes all his music. In so far as Tippett is religious, his is the humanistic religion of the divine latent in man (as proclaimed by Nietzsche and preached by Shaw), enriched by an empathy with the pantheism of the early romantics and with the unorthodox mysticism of such figures as Blake. Tippett had to struggle long and hard to win his vision; Messiaen's seems almost to have been born with him. In his music, Tippett most often achieves a state of ecstasy through a dense counterpoint of melismatic melody; in Messiaen, the melody is characteristically propelled into ecstasy by the luxuriant progressions of the underlying harmony, as for example in the 'Louange à l'Immortalité de Jésus' from the *Quatuor pour la Fin du Temps* of 1940–1. It is the difference of approach between the contrapuntalist (Tippett) and the harmonist (Messiaen). Despite their fundamental differences, there are moments when their voices are strikingly similar: to cite another example from the *Quatuor pour la Fin du Temps*, the 'Danse de la fureur, pour les sept trompettes', an unharmonized, unison melody in fast tempo and complex additive rhythms, makes a most interesting comparison with Tippett. Tippett and Messiaen are the only authentic visionaries amongst living composers, and each has produced some of the most life-enhancing music of our time.

Tippett's own solutions to two of the chief problems of twentieth-century music—the problem of language and the problem of move-ment—are, I believe, of great importance. Despite Schoenberg's assertion to the contrary, the musical language which he formulated and from which most currently fashionable styles are descended, is limited in expressive range. It is an ideal vehicle for the depiction of extreme emotional states: hence the total success of the monodrama *Erwartung*. It is hopelessly unsuited to comic opera: hence the total artistic failure of *Von Heute auf Morgen*. Of those composers who have used a Schoenbergian language, the most successful have been those who have expressionist things to say: Peter Maxwell Davies, for example. In short, serialism (under which blanket term one can broadly classify all styles ultimately derived from Schoenberg) cannot easily evoke states of joy, gaiety, exuberance. If composers still want to express such emotions in their music, they might profitably consider how Tippett's language in its development from orthodox tonality to pantonality has always been a potent vehicle for the widest range of expression. In the second place, Tippett, as has been mentioned, has continued to compose music which is not only in a fast tempo but whose harmonic progressions generate a real sense of dynamic move-ment. Within serialism it is hard to prevent genuine movement being clogged by a too densely chromatic harmony, and most composers faithful to this language can only create what amounts to a procession of static blocks, whether the tempo they specify is fast or slow.

As soon as we try to define Tippett's place in the history of twentieth-century music, we realize that he does not fit. He is a maverick (he has approvingly described Blake as such), an eccentric in the proper sense of the word. Our age is supposedly one in which artistic originality is sought after more keenly than ever before; yet much of the music of the present day is marked by a grey uniformity of expression (sometimes concealed by a surface gloss), as well as by a depressing lack of vitality. The international language of serialism has tended to foster these symptoms, and to provide an easy retreat from the rigours of developing a true artistic personality. Against this background, Tippett's exuberant individualism stands out in startling contrast. His music may sometimes disconcert, for Tippett has the true original's power to disturb. But it is certainly never conventional, and never superficial.

Tippett unashamedly assumes a prophetic role. Like his mentor Beethoven, he finds it an inseparable part of his calling to voice the aspirations of ordinary people; for, Tippett would claim, the artist has a deeper insight into the collective unconscious than most of us, and thus a surer understanding of our psychological needs. Tippett has taken upon himself the immense task of discovering new images of reconciliation and hope for a spiritually barren age; he wants, in his own words, 'to renew our sense of the comely and the beautiful. To create a dream.' That this is no unattainable aim is abundantly proved, I believe, by his music.

Bibliography

Michael Tippett: *Moving into Aquarius*, London, Routledge & Kegan Paul, 1959; enlarged paperback edition: London, Paladin Books, 1974.

Meirion Bowen, editor: *Music of the Angels—Essays and Sketchbooks of Michael Tippett*, London, Eulenberg Books, 1980.

Ian Kemp, editor: *Michael Tippett, A Symposium on his 60th Birthday*, London, Faber & Faber, 1965.
(Now out of print. A short biography, tributes from friends and a valuable selection of essays on the music. Includes a check-list of Tippett's writings.)

A Man of Our Time: an exhibition catalogue, London, Schott & Co, 1977. (Much documentary information including a complete list of Tippett's works, and a wide range of photographs.)

Michael Hurd: *Tippett*, in Novello Short Biographies, London, Novello & Co, 1978.

Eric Walter White: *Tippett and his Operas*, London, Barrie & Jenkins, 1979.

List of works mentioned in the text

(* = unpublished. A complete list of Tippett's music, published and un-published, can be found in *A Man of Our Time*, see Bibliography.)

c. 1928	*String Quartet in F minor
1928–30	*Concerto in D for flutes, oboe, horns and strings
1928	*String Quartet in F major (revised 1930)
1928	*Three Songs for voice and piano
	texts by Charlotte Mary Mew: 1. Sea Love 2. Afternoon Tea 3. Arracombe Wood
1929	*_The Village Opera_, Ballad Opera in 3 acts
	text and music written and arranged by the composer
1930	*Psalm in C: *The Gateway* for chorus and small orchestra
	text by Christopher Fry
1932	*String Trio in B flat
1933–4	*Symphony in B flat
1934	*_Robin Hood_, Ballad Opera
	dialogue by David Ayerst, lyrics by Ruth Pennyman
1934–5	String Quartet No. 1 (revised 1943)
1936–7	Sonata No. 1 for Piano (revised 1942 and 1954)
1937	*_A Song of Liberty_ for chorus and orchestra
	text from 'The Marriage of Heaven and Hell' by William Blake
1938	*_Robert of Sicily_, Opera for Children
	text by Christopher Fry adapted from Robert Downing, music arranged by the composer
1938–9	Concerto for Double String Orchestra
1939	*_Seven at One Stroke_, A Play for Children
	text by Christopher Fry, music arranged by the composer
1939–41	*Fantasia on a Theme of Handel* for Piano and Orchestra
1939–41	*A Child of Our Time*, Oratorio for SATB soloists, chorus and orchestra
	text by the composer
1941–2	String Quartet No. 2 in F sharp
1942	Two Madrigals for unaccompanied chorus SATB
	1. The Windhover (Gerald Manley Hopkins) 2. The Source (Edward Thomas)
1943	*Boyhood's End*, Cantata for tenor and piano
	text by W. H. Hudson
1943	*Plebs Angelica*, Motet for double chorus
1944–5	Symphony No. 1

1945–6   String Quartet No. 3

1946–52   *The Midsummer Marriage*, Opera in 3 acts
text by the composer

1950–1   *The Heart's Assurance*, Song Cycle for high voice and piano
texts by Sidney Keyes and Alun Lewis

1952   *Dance, Clarion Air*, Madrigal for five voices SSATB
text by Christopher Fry

1953   *Fantasia Concertante on a Theme of Corelli* for string orchestra

1953–5   Concerto for Piano and Orchestra

1955   Sonata for Four Horns

1956–7   Symphony No. 2

1958   *Crown of the Year*, Cantata for chorus SSA and instrumental
ensemble
text by Christopher Fry

1958–61   *King Priam*, Opera in 3 acts
text by the composer

1961   *Songs for Achilles* for tenor and guitar
texts by the composer: 1. In the Tent 2. Across the Plain 3. By the
Sea

1961   *Magnificat and Nunc Dimittis* for chorus SATB and organ

1962   Sonata No. 2 for Piano

1962   *Songs for Ariel* for voice and piano (or harpsichord)
texts by Shakespeare: 1. Come unto these Yellow Sands 2. Full
Fathom Five 3. Where the Bee Sucks

1962   *Praeludium* for brass, bells and percussion

1962–3   Concerto for Orchestra

1963–5   *The Vision of Saint Augustine* for baritone solo, chorus and
orchestra

1965–70   *The Shires Suite* for chorus and orchestra

1966–70   *The Knot Garden*, Opera in 3 acts
text by the composer

1970   *Songs for Dov* for tenor and small orchestra
texts by the composer

1970–2   Symphony No. 3 for soprano and orchestra
texts by the composer

1972–3   Sonata No. 3 for Piano

1973–6   *The Ice Break*, Opera in 3 acts
text by the composer

1976–7   Symphony No. 4

1977–8   String Quartet No. 4

Tippett's music is published by Schott & Co Ltd.

Index